Celebration Series

Lessons from History for Christian Living

Editorial Staff

Richard M. Davis . . . . .Editor
P. D. Buford . . . . .Associate Editor

Editor in Chief
United Pentecostal Church International

Robin Johnston

Writers

Lorin Bradbury	David W. King
C. A. Brewer	Daniel J. Koren
Richard M. Davis	David L. Reynolds
Rex Deckard	Charles A. Rutter
Doug Ellingsworth	Rodney Shaw
David Huston	Carl Trapani
Barry King	

Curriculum Committee

James E. Boatman	Jack C. Garrison
Donald Bryan	G. W. Hassebrock
P. D. Buford	Robin Johnston
Daniel L. Butler	David L. Reynolds
Steve L. Cannon	Charles A. Rutter
Richard M. Davis	Rick L. Wyser

God's Word is never outdated, outmoded, or irrelevant. It will provide direction and understanding for every generation. Times change and people change, but their fundamental needs are forever the same.

—Lesson 13, page 48

Adult Student Handbook

Spring 2013

Table of Contents

WORD AFLAME PUBLICATIONS
United Pentecostal Church International

www.wordaflame.org

Adult Student Handbook

Editor: Richard M. Davis • Cover Design: Dennis Fiorini • Design: Karen Myers

Manufactured in USA, Spring 2013, 193321.

Lessons from History for Christian Living

Respect for Godly Leadership

Lesson Text

Numbers 11:16-17

16 And the LORD said unto Moses, Gather unto me seventy men of the elders of Israel, whom thou knowest to be the elders of the people, and officers over them; and bring them unto the tabernacle of the congregation, that they may stand there with thee.

17 And I will come down and talk with thee there: and I will take of the spirit which is upon thee, and will put it upon them; and they shall bear the burden of the people with thee, that thou bear it not thyself alone.

Numbers 12:1-3, 8-13

1 And Miriam and Aaron spake against Moses because of the Ethiopian woman whom he had married: for he had married an Ethiopian woman.

2 And they said, Hath the LORD indeed spoken only by Moses? hath he not spoken also by us? And the LORD heard it.

3 (Now the man Moses was very meek, above all the men which were upon the face of the earth.)

. . . . .

8 With him will I speak mouth to mouth, even apparently, and not in dark speeches; and the similitude of the LORD shall he behold: wherefore then were ye not afraid to speak against my servant Moses?

9 And the anger of the LORD was kindled against them; and he departed.

10 And the cloud departed from off the tabernacle; and, behold, Miriam became leprous, white as snow: and Aaron looked upon Miriam, and, behold, she was leprous.

11 And Aaron said unto Moses, Alas, my lord, I beseech thee, lay not the sin upon us, wherein we have done foolishly, and wherein we have sinned.

12 Let her not be as one dead, of whom the flesh is half consumed when he cometh out of his mother's womb.

13 And Moses cried unto the LORD, saying, Heal her now, O God, I beseech thee.

Focus Thought

Respect for godly leadership is ordained by God and necessary for spiritual growth.

Focus Verse

Hebrews 13:17

Obey them that have the rule over you, and submit yourselves: for they watch for your souls, as they that must give account, that they may do it with joy, and not with grief: for that is unprofitable for you.

3

Why Respect Godly Leaders?
by Richard M. Davis

In a culture in which respect has been dramatically devalued, undermined, and discarded, why should believers bother to respect their godly leaders within the church? First, the Bible commands us to respect others and especially our leaders. For instance, see Philippians 2:3; I Timothy 5:17; I Thessalonians 5:12-13. But beyond the sense of biblical propriety and duty, it is just the right thing to do in order to bring order, progress, and advancement to the operation of the Lord's church on earth.

In his article "Godly Leadership—Introduction—Part 1," Brent Riggs offers some very good reasons we should respect our godly leaders:

• "A Godly leader is primarily someone who imitates Christ so that those who follow will become more like Christ. If I had to sum up leadership, that would be it. I Corinthians 11:1

• "A leader is someone who will choose right, act right, think right and seek what is right so that others may follow them to what is right. Luke 6:39

• "A leader is someone who will purposefully cultivate Godly character in their own life in order to instill it into the lives of those whom they lead. Ephesians 4:24

• "Leadership is having the courage to seek out and obey God and show others how to do the same in a world where very few seek God. Matthew 7:13" (*www.seriousfaith.com*, accessed March 21, 2012).

These few characteristics of godly leaders should be reason enough for honest and sincere believers to want to respect and follow them. God gave godly leadership as a gift to the church. We would be ungrateful and arrogant not to gracefully receive and appreciate the gift, which necessitates respect on our part.

Contemplating the Topic

Respect is a rare quality in the postmodern world. However, almost twenty centuries ago Jesus prescribed the remedy for the disease that attacks respect: "Do unto others, as you would have others do unto you." We show respect by giving others genuine, positive regard, listening to them with undivided attention, and acknowledging them as fellow human beings of value and worth. Conversely, withholding or manipulating these responses shows disrespect. Left unattended, disrespect becomes contempt and then full-blown hatred.

Searching the Scriptures

I. GODLY LEADERSHIP

A. Characteristics of Godly Leaders

Paul, in I Timothy 3:1-7, outlines the qualifications for one kind of godly leader, a bishop.
• Blameless
• Husband of one wife
• Vigilant
• Sober
• Of good behavior
• Given to hospitality
• Apt to teach
• Not given to wine
• No striker
• Not greedy of filthy lucre
• Patient
• Not a brawler
• Not covetous
• One that ruleth well
• Not a novice
• Has a good report of them who are outside

The New Testament gives several other characteristics required of those in church leadership, which conveys the principle that God holds leaders to high standards of conduct. Their willingness to accept and attempt to live up to these standards should automatically garner them the highest respect from those whom they lead.

B. Purpose of Godly Leaders

The standards for godly leaders are high because of the tremendous responsibility God places on them. Their charge is to lead the church in spiritual paths to higher levels of commitment and service. Paul declared that the purpose of godly leadership was "for the perfecting of the saints, for the work of the ministry, for the edifying of the body of Christ." (See Ephesians 4:11-12.)

II. WHY RESPECT GODLY LEADERS?

Today's society is quick to criticize those in leadership, and with criticism comes lack of respect. Admittedly, while there are times when criticism seems justified, we must never criticize any leader to the point of disrespecting his or her God-given office. Rather than criticizing leaders, let us pray for them. Paul exhorted "that, first of all, supplications, prayers, intercessions, and giving of thanks, be made for all men; for kings, and for all that are in authority; that we may lead a quiet and peaceable life in all godliness and honesty. For this is good and acceptable in the sight of God our Saviour" (I Timothy 2:1-3).

A. God Requires It

God expects His people to follow respectfully those He has appointed to lead them. "Obey them that have the rule over you, and submit yourselves: for they watch for your souls, as they that must give account, that they may do it with joy, and not with grief: for that is unprofitable for you" (Hebrews 13:17). Paul underscored the importance of this admonition in his letter to the Romans.

God's requirement of showing respect toward those in leadership is not arbitrary or conditional; it is an inviolate principle He expects us to follow consistently.

B. The Scriptures Reveal It

Many biblical events illustrate what happens when a person disrespects and disobeys godly leaders. Numbers 12:2 records the first instance of disrespect shown toward Moses' leadership. Moses' siblings, Aaron and Miriam, criticized their younger brother. "Hath the LORD indeed spoken only by Moses? hath he not spoken also by us?" God rebuked and punished them for their critical disrespect. In a twinkling Miriam's body became infected with leprosy. She was not healed until Moses, the object of her scorn, interceded with God for her.

Numbers 16 describes another incident of rebellion when Korah and a large number of influential Israelites challenged Moses' right to lead. The Lord punished them swiftly and fatally: "The earth opened her mouth, and swallowed them up" (Numbers 16:32).

To counterbalance these incidents of disrespect, Exodus 18 describes what happened when Jethro, Moses' father-in-law, came for a visit to the Israelite camp. He observed Moses sitting as the sole arbiter surrounded by a milling crowd, many of whom waited all day in the hot sun for their turn to present their case. Jethro remonstrated, "Why try to handle all of these cases yourself? Look at the chaos—it wears everyone out. You can't bear this heavy load much longer."

Jethro advised Moses to choose capable men of truth who could teach the people godly ordinances and advise them which way to go. "If thou shalt do this thing, and God command thee so, then thou shalt be able to endure, and all this people shall also go to their place in peace" (Exodus 18:23). Moses followed Jethro's advice, and these leaders bore the burden with Moses, "[judging] the people at all seasons: the hard causes they brought unto Moses, but every small matter they judged themselves" (Exodus 18:26).

C. The Church Needs It

Church members need to show respect for their leaders. Criticism and disrespect can kill a revival spirit, but respect and enthusiastic support for leadership enhances the spiritual atmosphere. Paul wrote, "Follow me as I follow Christ." The church of today should take up that challenge.

III. DANGER OF REJECTING GODLY LEADERSHIP

A. Creates Division

Disrespecting certain godly leaders and disfavoring others is divisive and goes against the will and plan of God for His church. Paul's first letter to the Corinthians declared, "God is not the author of confusion" (I Corinthians 14:33) and admonished the church to be united, not divided. This reproof was prompted by the factions in the church at Corinth: one camp claimed to be following after Paul's leadership, another camp after Apollos's, another after Cephas's, and yet others who claimed to be following Christ (I Corinthians 1:10-13). In choosing one leader over another they had become divided and contentious, and Paul realized that unless these schisms were healed, the other disorders discussed in I Corinthians could not be remedied.

B. Disrupts Progress

When partiality is shown toward one particular individual or group in the church, it causes division and hurt. This disrupts the progress of the church. Things that disrupt spiritual unity and growth are definitely not from God. They should be seen as the work of the enemy. In Matthew 13:24-30 Jesus described the enemy (Satan) as sowing weeds among the wheat to diminish the harvest. Jesus told this parable to illustrate how the devil does whatever he can to hinder the growth and progress of the church.

C. Brings God's Judgment

Satan may sow weeds and try to disrupt God's plan for a mighty harvest of souls, but eventually there will be a day of reckoning and judgment upon the unrepentant and disobedient. The Israelites' disrespect of Moses brought punishment and plague (Numbers 16:41-50). King Saul's usurpation of the sacred priestly duties resulted in the loss of his kingdom (I Samuel 13:5-14). When Ananias and Sapphira lied to their apostolic leaders, God sent swift judgment and they died (Acts 5:1-11).

IV. RESPECT REWARDED

A. Brings Personal Satisfaction

Our respect for others breeds respect from others. Each of us is worthy of respect simply because of our basic humanity and our membership in the body of Christ. Showing respect for others by acknowledging their place in God's family also promotes a heartfelt connection to them. We are one body made up of many parts. Each member shares a connection to the whole, and all the various parts operate under the headship of Jesus Christ. It feels good to be part of something worthwhile—and there is nothing more worthwhile than the church of God!

B. Blessed by God

God blesses us when we submit to those who have the rule over us. Submission acknowledges the important place godly leaders have in our lives. People in leadership positions can lead by force, by charisma, or by example, but rarely do we think about them leading by submission. However, Jesus turned things upside down. Instead of a lecture on the subject of submission, He impressed the concept into the core of their being when he washed His followers' dirty feet (John 13:4-17). This act modeled the underlying principle of godly leadership: just as He, the Son of God, came to serve, so should they.

Submission is the key to unity and harmony in human relationships and is at the core of man's relationship with God. A blessing comes to us when we submit to those in authority (I Peter 2:13-3:7).

C. Unifies the Church

The church began on the Day of Pentecost when the disciples, united in mind and purpose in the upper room in Jerusalem, waited for the fulfillment of Jesus' promise. (See Acts 2:1, 42, 44-46.)

Respect for other believers breeds love, and love breeds unity. God wants His church to be united. A united church is solid and strong, a formidable force that confronts and conquers the opposition of the devil and the world. Jesus Christ promised that even the "gates of hell shall not prevail against it" (Matthew 16:18).

D. Fosters Revival

The unity of the early church created and sustained a revival atmosphere that grew until it permeated the whole world. The respect shown to the disciples and other church leaders was a key ingredient in making the church a universal entity. This respect came from unbelievers as well as believers, and it led to revival. (See Acts 2:42-43; 4:33; 5:12; 8:6.)

Respect for those God has placed over us in leadership will please the Lord. Showing proper respect brings us closer to the fount of apostolic revival.

Internalizing the Message

Here are some key points to take home today.
• God has established positions of authority and leadership in every area of human interaction, including the church.
• Godly leaders are all called to minister and serve the church in a variety of capacities.
• It is God's will for us to subject ourselves willingly to those over us and show proper respect to those in godly leadership.
• Lack of respect often comes from personal pride and an unwillingness to acknowledge others as being over us.
• God wants us to work together harmoniously as a unified body under His headship to accomplish His will.
• Showing proper respect sets a good example and brings revival and other blessings.

From the Wilderness to Jordan

2
week of
03.10.13

Lesson Text

Numbers 14:26-27, 29, 31-33, 38

26 And the LORD spake unto Moses and unto Aaron, saying,

27 How long shall I bear with this evil congregation, which murmur against me? I have heard the murmurings of the children of Israel, which they murmur against me.

. . . . .

29 Your carcases shall fall in this wilderness; and all that were numbered of you, according to your whole number, from twenty years old and upward, which have murmured against me.

. . . . .

31 But your little ones, which ye said should be a prey, them will I bring in, and they shall know the land which ye have despised.

32 But as for you, your carcases, they shall fall in this wilderness.

33 And your children shall wander in the wilderness forty years, and bear your whoredoms, until your carcases be wasted in the wilderness.

. . . . .

38 But Joshua the son of Nun, and Caleb the son of Jephunneh, which were of the men that went to search the land, lived still.

Focus Thought

God is faithful to give strength, guidance, and protection to those who are determined to endure to the end.

Focus Verse

Romans 6:23

For the wages of sin is death; but the gift of God is eternal life through Jesus Christ our Lord.

From the Wilderness to Jordan
by Gary D. Erickson

Life is like an arduous journey through a wilderness. We are forced to cut our way through thick vegetation, cross rivers, climb mountains, and fight threatening predators. Life is filled with opportunities as well as pitfalls. Sometimes we detour around things and sometimes persevere through them. Sometimes we triumph over our obstacles and sometimes we suffer defeat. Nevertheless, we forge on. We cannot opt out even if we want to. Time moves on and we move with it.

God has provided all we need to make our journey a success. The Bible is our map and the Holy Spirit is our inspiration and empowerment. Sometimes there are well-worn paths that make our progress smooth, and at other times we have to cut our way through uncharted jungle and up the sides of steep cliffs. The perils are many and the obstacles are real, but life is an exhilarating challenge!

God made us for the challenge. Some people climb Mt. Everest, others swim the English Channel, and others sail around the world in a yacht. We may not be so adventurous, but everyone needs a challenge. It is what makes life meaningful. The challenge gives us opportunity to engage our talents and abilities. It gives us the opportunity to triumph over opposition. God built us for the rigors of the challenge.

Living the Christian life is one of the most challenging undertakings. It will not be easy, but the rewards are amazing. Jesus said, "These things I have spoken unto you, that in me ye might have peace. In the world ye shall have tribulation: but be of good cheer; I have overcome the world" (John 16:33). Because He overcame, we can overcome as well.

Contemplating the Topic

Unbelief and rebellion have robbed many people of the blessings and promises of God. Admittedly, God's promises often are attained only with persistent grappling with giants, "squatters" who want to keep us from obtaining what rightfully belongs to us. But the Lord is faithful, and His promises await those who endure. Let us make correct choices, refuse to return to Egypt, and press onward to the victories God has prepared for His people.

Searching the Scriptures

I. THE REPORT OF THE SPIES

A. The Faithless Report

In accordance with God's command, Moses chose an influential man from each of the twelve tribes to scout out the land. God hoped their discoveries of the beauty and plenty of the land would inspire faith in His promises. He said, "Be ye of good courage" (Numbers 13:20).

The Hebrew words translated "courage" or "courageous" could have many connotations: steadfastly minded, fortified, established, or obstinate. But most important was to go in "the strength of Jah" or Yahweh (*The Complete Word Study Old Testament*). God desired Israel's confidence in His power to conquer, whether the opponent be Egypt, Canaan, or any other foe. However, only two of the spies approached the mission with courageous determination. Although the other ten appreciated the good land, their courage shriveled when they saw the massive walled cities inhabited by the children of Anak (giants), Amalekites, Hittites, Jebusites, Amorites, and Canaanites.

Preferring the known to the unknown, the people decided to return to Egypt. They did not consider that if they turned back, God in His displeasure might not continue to protect and lead them with the pillar of cloud and fire. If they went forward into Canaan they could die. If they went backward to Egypt without water, food, and protection, they surely would die. Their weeping, complaining, and rebellion pushed God to the brink of destroying them.

B. The Faithful Report

Numbers 13:3-15 gives a detailed list of the names of the twelve spies, but today only two of the names—Joshua and Caleb—are remembered, because of their good report.

C. The People's Response

The same people who had vowed to fulfill their obligations to the covenant with God now cast it aside. Instead of enjoying the blessings of the covenant, they would suffer its curses. God decided to grant their death wish.

The people must have felt a pang of fear when the glory of the Lord billowed up out of the Tabernacle. Moses and Aaron fell on their faces in anguish, in full view of the congregation. God said, "How long will this people provoke me? and how long will it be ere they believe me, for all the signs which I have shewed among them? I will smite them with the pestilence, and disinherit them, and will make of thee a greater nation and mightier than they" (Numbers 14:11-12).

Ignoring the honor of the Lord's intention to found a new nation through him, Moses "stood in the gap," serving as a shield from divine wrath. Such pleas coming from this man whom the Lord knew "face to face" began to allay His wrath. (See Ezekiel 22:30-31; Deuteronomy 34:10.)

Moses reminded God of His own description of His character as loving, longsuffering, merciful, and forgiving. He begged God to pardon and forgive His people.

D. God's Response

Even though the people had provoked God "ten times" (Numbers 14:22), because of Moses' intercession, God pardoned the people. Yet He refused to change His mind about the people who had seen the glory and the miracles in Egypt. Everyone from the ages of twenty and up—except Joshua and Caleb—would die under a curse. "Your carcases shall fall in this wilderness. . . . [and] your little ones, which ye said should be a prey, them will I bring in, and they shall know the land which ye have despised" (Numbers 14:29, 31).

II. THE WILDERNESS JOURNEY

A. God's Guidance

Because of failure to accept and believe the promises of God, Israel wandered in the wilderness for forty years, one year for each day the spies had reconnoitered the Land of Promise. In spite of Israel's faithlessness, God continued to guide and protect them with a pillar of cloud by day and a pillar of fire by night. When the cloud moved, they pulled up stakes and followed it to the next encampment. Through these gifts of grace, God was attempting to teach the people that if they

could trust Him to take care of them in the wilderness, they could trust He would fulfill His promise to give them a land flowing with milk and honey.

One would think enough rebellions and swift punishments had occurred to preclude any further attempts to usurp Moses and Aaron's authority. But a Levite named Korah (Numbers 16:1), who did not think his position was lofty enough, rose up against Moses' civil authority and Aaron's priestly authority. Dathan, Abiram, and On, descendents of Reuben, took part in his rebellion.

After several confrontations, the entire congregation gathered to see whom the Lord would vindicate—Moses and Aaron, or Korah and his followers. Moses told the people to stand back, and the earth opened its mouth and swallowed the leaders of the rebellion, and fire from the Lord devoured the 250 men who had offered incense. Thus, to oppose and despise Moses and Aaron was to oppose and despise God, who had placed the prophet and the priest in authority.

B. God's Provision

For forty years God continued to send manna until they entered the Promised Land and ate of the crops that sat in the fields. (See Joshua 5:12.) Perhaps the women grew weary of wearing the same garments for forty years, because their clothes and sandals did not wear out. (See Deuteronomy 29:5.)

Although at times Israel complained they did not have anything to drink or any variety of foods to eat, Moses said, "The LORD thy God hath blessed thee . . . he knoweth thy walking through this great wilderness: these forty years the LORD thy God hath been with thee; thou hast lacked nothing" (Deuteronomy 2:7).

But Israel often did not see it that way. At Kadesh, toward the end of their journey, they complained so bitterly about the lack of water, grain, and fruit that Moses and Aaron fell upon their faces before the Lord. God told Moses to take his rod and speak to the rock, a variation of the command to strike the rock soon after they left Egypt (Exodus 17:6).

Moses had spent the prime of his life leading the people. Perhaps he thought the struggle might be for nothing if the people, like their fathers, turned back again. His frustration boiled over and lifting the rod he said, "Hear now, ye rebels; must we fetch you water out of this rock?" (Numbers 20:10), and he struck the rock twice in the sight of the congregation. It was the only known time it could not be written, "Thus did Moses: according to all that the LORD commanded him, so did he" (Exodus 40:16). Because of this sin neither Moses nor Aaron entered the Promised Land. The man who preached faithfully God's message of deliverance and promise to Israel was only allowed to view it from Mount Nebo.

C. God's Protection

Israel's first encounter was with the Edomites, whose land sprawled across the direct route from the wilderness to their destination east of the Jordan River. Moses approached the Edomites with great tact, calling them "brothers" and expressing why they wanted safe passage through the land. But the hatred of Edom for Israel, which had begun in Genesis 27:41, still burned and they threatened to attack. Israel began a detour around Edom and came to Mount Hor on the northwest border between Edom and Canaan, where Aaron died.

III. THE REWARD OF ENDURANCE

A. Arrival at the Jordan

When God told Moses his life was nearly over, Moses asked God to appoint a successor. "And the LORD said unto Moses, Take thee Joshua the son of Nun, a man in whom is the spirit, and lay thine hand upon him; and set him before Eleazar the priest, and before all the congregation; and give him a charge in their sight. And thou shalt put some of thine honour upon him, that all the congregation of the children of Israel may be obedient" (Numbers 27:18-20). Then, after much teaching and admonition, Moses died.

Israel's wandering came to an end on the banks of the Jordan River. The Lord spoke to Joshua and gave him the same promises He had given Moses. He encouraged him to be strong and courageous, for Joshua, as one of the twelve spies, had seen the giants and the fortified cities they were about to invade. He knew he could not do it on Israel's strength alone. He would have to trust that God would bring it to pass.

B. Preparation for Crossing

Joshua told the people to prepare food, for they would soon pass over Jordan and go in to possess the land. On the eve of the river crossing Joshua instructed the people and the priests, "Sanctify yourselves: for to morrow the LORD will do wonders among you" (Joshua 3:5).

An air of excitement and nervous apprehension filled the camp. Joshua said, "The living God is among you, and . . . he will without fail drive out from before you" the people of the land. (See Joshua 3:10.) The river was at flood stage (Joshua 3:15), but Joshua prepared them for what would happen during the crossing. The priests would take up the Ark of the Covenant and head for the river. When the soles of their feet dipped into the water, it would begin to back up in a heap and the people would cross over on dry land.

Everything Joshua said came to pass. The priests stood in the middle of the river bearing the Ark while the people passed on either side. Joshua asked twelve men, one from each tribe, to take up a stone from the midst of the river and carry up it to the western bank. When everyone had passed over safely, the priests crossed. As soon as their feet stood on the western bank, the waters resumed their flow and flooded the banks as they had before.

That night in the encampment, the twelve men erected a memorial with the twelve stones. It would serve to teach future generations that God keeps His promises.

C. Promise Fulfilled

In three swift campaigns Joshua overtook key cities in central, southern, and northern Palestine. The allocation of the land occurred sometime toward the end of Joshua's life. It is described in great detail in chapters 13-21 of the Book of Joshua. It confirmed to Israel that faith and obedience will bring full possession of the land. Their forefathers' doubt and disobedience had kept them from realizing the inheritance that came to their children.

Internalizing the Message

We can learn valuable lessons from contrasting these two generations of Israelites we have discussed today. The first generation grew up with resentment for Egyptian authority and seemed to transfer the same resentment to Moses' authority.

As the second generation grew up, the teaching of Moses and Aaron had taken root in their hearts. They believed the messages they heard about the promises of God. Their strong desire to obtain the promises propelled them into the Promised Land where they conquered the giants and their walled cities and obtained an inheritance.

Triumph of Training

3
week of
03.17.13

Lesson Text

Judges 2:7-17

7 And the people served the LORD all the days of Joshua, and all the days of the elders that outlived Joshua, who had seen all the great works of the LORD, that he did for Israel.

8 And Joshua the son of Nun, the servant of the LORD, died, being an hundred and ten years old.

9 And they buried him in the border of his inheritance in Timnath-heres, in the mount of Ephraim, on the north side of the hill Gaash.

10 And also all that generation were gathered unto their fathers: and there arose another generation after them, which knew not the LORD, nor yet the works which he had done for Israel.

11 And the children of Israel did evil in the sight of the LORD, and served Baalim:

12 And they forsook the LORD God of their fathers, which brought them out of the land of Egypt, and followed other gods, of the gods of the people that were round about them, and bowed themselves unto them, and provoked the LORD to anger.

13 And they forsook the LORD, and served Baal and Ashtaroth.

14 And the anger of the LORD was hot against Israel, and he delivered them into the hands of spoilers that spoiled them, and he sold them into the hands of their enemies round about, so that they could not any longer stand before their enemies.

15 Whithersoever they went out, the hand of the LORD was against them for evil, as the LORD had said, and as the LORD had sworn unto them: and they were greatly distressed.

16 Nevertheless the LORD raised up judges, which delivered them out of the hand of those that spoiled them.

17 And yet they would not hearken unto their judges, but they went a whoring after other gods, and bowed themselves unto them: they turned quickly out of the way which their fathers walked in, obeying the commandments of the LORD; but they did not so.

Focus Thought

If the blessings of God are to continue, each generation must teach godly principles to the next generation.

Focus Verse

II Timothy 2:2

And the things that thou hast heard of me among many witnesses, the same commit thou to faithful men, who shall be able to teach others also.

11

Passing the Baton
by Gary D. Erickson

The Olympics are a convergence of the greatest athletes in the world. Competing men and women dream about winning the gold medallion and standing on the winner's platform. Years of training and preparation are invested in this grandest of competitions. One of the signature events in the Summer Olympics is the relay race. Teams of runners work together by passing the baton from one runner to the other. The speed of the runners is important, but the transition of the baton must be flawless. If the baton is dropped, the team is automatically disqualified. Passing the baton is critical.

The USA teams have traditionally been a dominant presence in the Olympics. The 2008 games in Beijing brought the USA teams an embarrassing defeat in the 100-meter relay races. "The once mighty USA sprint team officially hit rock bottom when both the men's and women's 4x100m relay teams dropped their batons in a night of drama in Beijing's Bird's Nest stadium. . . . The same thing happened in Athens four years ago with the USA women's team failing to get the baton around in the final, handing Jamaica the gold medal" (*Foxsports.com*, August 21, 2008). Running fast alone will not win the race. The baton must be brought safely across the finish line.

We can be just as careless spiritually. Running well in life's race is a great achievement, but we must pass the baton to the next generation. Discipling and mentoring others is vital to the preservation of the church. Paul said, "Holding forth the word of life; that I may rejoice in the day of Christ, that I have not run in vain, neither laboured in vain" (Philippians 2:16). We are always one generation from extinction.

Contemplating the Topic

Joshua and Caleb, the only two survivors from what we will call the "First Generation" to escape Egyptian bondage, possessed unfeigned faith. Their faith enabled them to cross over into the Promised Land. The faith of the next generation, which we will call the "Second Generation," may at first have been unfeigned and strong enough to propel them into the Promised Land, but they failed to follow through in faith by driving out all the Canaanites from their inheritance. Their laxity and dabbling in the worship of Baal and Ashtaroth caused the next generation, which we will call the "Third Generation," to grow up without any role models of faith, integrity, and love of the one true God. They failed to follow through on Moses' admonition to their forefathers.

The absence of faith set the Third Generation adrift from its traditional moorings. They intermarried with the nations around them and adopted their gods and lifestyles. God in His anger withdrew His blessings and allowed these same nations to harass and to dominate them. It was a dark time in the history of Israel, a time of apostasy, covenant disobedience, and religious syncretism.

Searching the Scriptures

I. THE FIRST GENERATION

Stiffnecked and faithless, this generation provoked God throughout the entire forty years in the wilderness—all except Joshua and Caleb, the two men who figuratively stood head and shoulders above the rest. (See Numbers 26:65.) They were upright, courageous, zealous for God, and obedient to Moses. Moses recognized these traits in Joshua and mentored him for future leadership of Israel. We can follow the progression of Joshua's developing spirituality and leadership by following the chain of Scripture verses where his name appears.

We first hear Joshua's name mentioned when he led the Israelites to victory over Amalek (Exodus 17:10), the battle during which Aaron and Hur upheld Moses' arms so Israel could prevail. After the battle, God told Moses to write about it in a book for a memorial and read it in Joshua's hearing (Exodus 17:14). God wanted His Word implanted in Joshua's heart.

Toward the end of his life Joshua could not help but observe the beginning of a generational drift. True to the Lord's command,

12

Joshua had led three fierce campaigns that conquered key areas of Canaan, leaving with each tribe the responsibility to destroy or drive out the inhabitants who lived within the borders of their inheritance. However, the next generation failed to do so. (See Judges 1:17-36.)

II. THE SECOND GENERATION

A. Ignored Responsibilities

The elders of the Second Generation promised Joshua they would always serve God, but their faith was built on the knowledge of the blessings and provision of God, never on a personal relationship with Him. To them their faith was only a "responsibility."

B. Failed to Teach the Young

God expected the Second Generation to teach and train their children in the history of their people and in the ways of God. However, any attempt to instruct or command would have profited little because they themselves did not live by the pattern of sincerity, genuineness, and truthfulness. How could the children believe their parents were serious, and wish to obey them, so long as their actions contradicted their instructions?

C. Vision Clouded

The Second Generation lost sight of God's plan for their lives and turned to other lifestyles, other covenants, and other gods. Their apostasy was a "fundamental and revolutionary perversion of a correct understanding of the world" (*Zondervan Bible Commentary*, 2008).

III. THE THIRD GENERATION

A. Knew Not God

The Third Generation "knew not the LORD, nor yet the works which he had done for Israel" (Judges 2:10).

This generational drift happened too often in Israel. David had a passion for God and His Word, and was an extravagant worshiper. But he failed to train his sons in the ways of God. As they grew, they committed gross sins.

B. Products of the Failing Faith of Their Fathers

Although Israel forgot God, God did not forget His people. When the Third Generation cried out to Him for help, He sent a leader who delivered them from their oppressors and led them to victory. All too soon, however, they forgot the reason for their peace and prosperity and fell back into the lifestyle of their neighbors—only to have the cycle begin all over again.

IV. THE REVIVED GENERATION

A. Strength from the Past

God planned that Israel would keep their identity and faith alive by meditating upon their history and the Word of God, by living it, and by rehearsing it to their children.

However, they failed to pass their faith from generation to generation. Consequently, they suffered from evil leaders who only led them farther and farther away from God. Eventually, the voice of God fell silent for four hundred years. As a nation, they suffered from complete separation from God.

In the fullness of time, God began once again to work His plan through Israel— through John the Baptist, the birth of Jesus Christ, the apostles, and the birth of the church. They became a Revived Generation, which continues through the church until today.

B. Steadfast in the Present

Some in our generation are third- or fourth- or fifth-generation Pentecostals. We can keep the unfeigned faith alive in the same way God commanded Israel: to believe it, to live it, and to teach it to our children. However, we have an advantage over the Israelites. We have the power of the Holy Spirit to help us keep that which God and our elders have committed to us.

C. Vision for the Future

We have the great responsibility to pass on our faith to the next generation. As parents and teachers we must have the wisdom and vision to know the correct path for our children. It is not about what we *want* for them, but what is *right and good* in God's sight.

Internalizing the Message

The New Covenant community, like the Old, is confronted by choices. We can either be distracted by conforming to the world around us, or we can commit to loving Jesus in covenant obedience. We have the same mandate as Israel to pass on our faith and heritage to the next generation. If we do not, we are violating our covenant vows

4
week of
03.24.13

Committed, Not Conceited

Lesson Text

Judges 4:4-9

4 And Deborah, a prophetess, the wife of Lapidoth, she judged Israel at that time.

5 And she dwelt under the palm tree of Deborah between Ramah and Bethel in mount Ephraim: and the children of Israel came up to her for judgment.

6 And she sent and called Barak the son of Abinoam out of Kedesh-naphtali, and said unto him, Hath not the LORD God of Israel commanded, saying, Go and draw toward mount Tabor, and take with thee ten thousand men of the children of Naphtali and of the children of Zebulun?

7 And I will draw unto thee to the river Kishon Sisera, the captain of Jabin's army, with his chariots and his multitude; and I will deliver him into thine hand.

8 And Barak said unto her, If thou wilt go with me, then I will go: but if thou wilt not go with me, then I will not go.

9 And she said, I will surely go with thee: notwithstanding the journey that thou takest shall not be for thine honour; for the LORD shall sell Sisera into the hand of a woman. And Deborah arose, and went with Barak to Kedesh.

Judges 5:1-2, 11-12

1 Then sang Deborah and Barak the son of Abinoam on that day, saying,

2 Praise ye the LORD for the avenging of Israel, when the people willingly offered themselves.

. . . . .

11 They that are delivered from the noise of archers in the places of drawing water, there shall they rehearse the righteous acts of the LORD, even the righteous acts toward the inhabitants of his villages in Israel: then shall the people of the LORD go down to the gates.

12 Awake, awake, Deborah: awake, awake, utter a song: arise, Barak, and lead thy captivity captive, thou son of Abinoam.

Focus Thought

Committed leaders work together in unity to ensure a successful outcome for the work of God.

Focus Verse

I Corinthians 3:9

For we are labourers together with God: ye are God's husbandry, ye are God's building.

Committed, Not Conceited

by Gary D. Erickson

Successful leaders today are not necessarily extroverted, highly gifted, intelligent people who tower over the abilities of others. A leader is anyone who can inspire others to use their talents to get the job done. "Collaboration," "emotional intelligence," and "networking" are important. A career advisor told me that job interviews today are focused more on how well a prospective leader gets along with others. Knowledge and expertise are important, but having the ability to work with others is just as critical.

The corporate world is different from the church in many ways, but effective leadership principles are prevailing virtues—respect for others, teamwork, integrity, willingness to sacrifice, a good work ethic, communication skills, a positive attitude, and decisiveness. One of the most important virtues of a leader is the ability to work in unity with others, encouraging team members to use their talents toward achieving goals.

The church needs dedicated leaders today—leaders who are willing to network with the body of Christ and respect the opinions and gifts of others. By collaborating with other leaders, we multiply our own efforts. The very nature of Christianity places us in tandem with others.

Paul said we are a body fitly framed together—each individual serving a specific function in the body. God uses all kinds of people to get His job done and save the world. God used a woman named Deborah to defeat Israel's enemies. He used a shy man named Moses to lead the Hebrews to the Promised Land. He used a warrior named David to lead Israel as their king. He used a fisherman named Peter to be the presenter at Pentecost. He used a scholar named Paul to turn the world upside down with the gospel. He can use you as well! Stay connected to the body of Christ and your influence will grow.

Contemplating the Topic

Deborah and Barak's story illustrates powerfully that where there is strong, anointed leadership coupled with faithful workers properly aligned with godly leadership, great things can be achieved. It also shows that for every accomplishment all glory belongs to God.

Searching the Scriptures

I. A JUDGE IS CHOSEN

A. Diversity of Leadership

God's plan has always been to place godly, committed visionaries and leaders in front of His people, leaders who follow Him as their ultimate guide. (See Deuteronomy 32:7-10; Psalm 80:1; Isaiah 63:14; John 10:3.) Deborah was the fifth and only female judge in the history of the nation of Israel. This speaks of several things about God and His choosing of leadership. The first is that God understands timing for leadership is critical. Every generation is different and so are their needs. One generation needs a Moses to lead, another generation needs a David to lead, and still another generation will need a Samuel to lead.

B. Character of Leadership

The Scriptures describe the exploits of the mighty King David, who greatly expanded Israel's borders and subdued surrounding nations; the ministry of the prophet Jeremiah, whom a backslidden generation hated for telling them the truth; and the bravery of Queen Esther, who "came into the kingdom" at a crucial time in Jewish history. It is evident that Deborah's leadership matched a specific time and need as well, for under God's leadership she won a great victory for the nation.

We as Christians should understand that every leader has distinct leadership characteristics God desires to match to specific needs at specific times. Many Christians will follow and obey leadership only when they agree with and relate to it. This shows spiritual immaturity and personal pride. Our responsibility as Christian servants is to allow God to place in leadership those whom He knows can get the job done, and then simply follow and obey.

15

C. Commitment of Leadership

Many people, like Demas, readily become involved in the kingdom of God, but when it comes to committing themselves, they back away silently. They avoid doing anything that involves self-sacrifice. Jesus told a potential follower who wanted first to bid farewell to those at home, "No man, having put his hand to the plough, and looking back, is fit for the kingdom of God" (Luke 9:62). When God chooses followers and leaders, He always looks for commitment.

II. CHOOSING A COWORKER

Israel's first conflict with "Jabin king of Hazor" occurred in Joshua 11:1-13. At that time Jabin headed a coalition of Galilean city-states that tried unsuccessfully to thwart the Israelite invasion. Israel slew the inhabitants and burned the city to the ground. Archaeological evidence suggests that by the time of the judges, Jabin could have been a continuing representative of the old powerful coalition, now dominated by Sisera, captain of the host. Israel clearly feared Sisera's coalition and considered it an ongoing threat to their existence as a nation. When they cried to the Lord for help, He chose a woman to deliver them.

A. Deborah's Invitation

As a "mother in Israel" Deborah received prominence and respect. She stood as the only woman in the lineup of male judges, and the only one with whom prophecy is associated—until Samuel. The people of Israel "came up to her for judgment" (Judges 4:5). She knew she was not a warrior and therefore needed another strong leader to help her defeat the Canaanite coalition that had menaced Israel for twenty years. From her home in the south of Ephraim near the territory of Judah, Deborah sent an invitation to Barak who lived in the north, not far from the Sea of Galilee and possibly less than a hundred miles from Hazor. If Barak would add his special combat skills to Deborah's faith in God, they could unite and embolden the disjointed tribes and lead them to victory.

With the Great Commission, Jesus invited every believer to participate in His redemptive mission. (See Mark 16:15-16.) The passion, commitment, and invitation of spiritual leaders should inspire and unite believers to become committed and involved, and to keep working until the mission is complete. There is room for all to participate.

B. Barak's Response

Barak clearly was the man for the mission, but he needed the confidence Deborah's presence would bring. He drew confidence and direction from her vision, her faith, and her spiritual leadership.

Barak's call from Kedesh resulted in the assembling of ten thousand Israelite warriors in the region of Mount Tabor. Such a large detachment did not escape Sisera's notice, and he deployed nine hundred chariots, additional infantry, and support troops to the region.

C. Kindred Spirits

Visionary leaders need people who are willing to come alongside and work toward the completion of the task. When they work together, these second-level leaders can accomplish what visionaries cannot accomplish by themselves. Successful visionaries instill their vision in others, base their leadership on a positive picture of the future, and provide a clear sense of direction as to how to get there. Deborah directed Barak toward Mount Tabor, near the river Kishon, and assured that God would deliver Sisera into his hand (Judges 4:6-7). Visionary leaders inspire and energize people, giving them confidence that the vision will become reality.

Satan knows the potential of people who love each other and are working side by side. He will do everything in his power to shove a wedge in their unity to thwart the will of God. We can avoid disruptions by learning to recognize the work of the enemy and refusing to allow anything to come between us and our godly leadership. Sisera's self-assurance told him he would defeat Israel, but he did not factor in Israel's conquering God.

III. TEAM LEADERS

A. Driven by Commitment

The size and power of the foe did not deter Deborah, Barak, and their followers. The warriors were determined to follow where God led, whether they heard the message directly from God or from the leader. They advanced by faith and fought with all their might. Such faith engenders the intervention of God. They kept the vision in focus, expended the time and energy, believed God would do what He said He would do, and kept fighting until they achieved victory.

The lyrics of Deborah's song describe the unity among the people. "My heart is toward the governors of Israel, that offered themselves willingly among the people" (Judges 5:9). The Hebrew term "offered themselves" is related to the noun for "freewill offerings." (See Leviticus 7:16; 22:23.) The NIV renders the phrase, "When the leaders let their hair loose," which the *Evangelical Commentary of the Bible* (1989) explains was an "act of religious dedication in assuming leadership."

God searches among many possible leaders until He finds dedicated men and women filled with the Holy Ghost who can effect spiritual change in the world. Then He invites believers to get behind the leader and work to see the goal accomplished. Most Christians truly desire to do something for Jesus, but many lack the commitment to stay on task until the goal is realized. Our flesh wants attention and praise but rarely desires to pay the price of commitment. Leaders and followers alike must be willing to lay down their life, pick up their cross, and follow Jesus faithfully no matter where He leads. (See Matthew 16:24.)

B. No Personal Agendas

Barak said to Deborah, "I will go if you will go." Besides hesitancy, this also indicated his respect and trust in Deborah's leadership and his desire to work alongside her to accomplish God's will. The text does not say he protested that a woman would receive the glory for the victory. He did not change his mind and say he would face Sisera without Deborah's presence. Even if he did not receive the victor's reward, Barak still wanted to be a part of Israel's victory over the Canaanites and work toward the unity of Israel.

Leaders and followers cannot work effectively together if one of them has a personal agenda different from God's will. The kingdom of Heaven would be spared many distractions, heartaches, and spiritual fatalities if both Christian leaders and their followers kept personal agendas out of their spiritual calling. Paul beseeched, "Let us walk by the same rule, let us mind the same thing" (Philippians 3:16).

C. Unity Brings Victory

The song of Deborah underscores the importance of godly leadership. Victory cannot be achieved unless the leaders take the initiative, and then are joined by people who follow them willingly. (See Judges 5:2, 9.) Unity brings victory when workers embrace the will of God and refuse to lose sight of the vision of their God-chosen leader.

The outpouring of the Holy Ghost on the Day of Pentecost unified the church. "And by the hands of the apostles were many signs and wonders wrought among the people; (and they were all with one accord in Solomon's porch. And of the rest durst no man join himself to them: but the people magnified them. And believers were the more added to the Lord, multitudes both of men and women.)" (Acts 5:12-14). Like the people who esteemed the apostles highly (Acts 5:13), we should fear to be the one who disrupts the unity of the body of Christ.

Internalizing the Message

We must recognize and respond to clear, spiritual leadership when God provides it to the church. Spiritual authority is a vital issue with God, and it would benefit all believers to ensure their lives are aligned properly with their spiritual authority. When we see a visionary leader accomplishing great things, he or she is drawing on the resources of God and others who work alongside. The followers, through their appreciation and support of their leader, can develop and strengthen the leader's qualities in themselves.

A battle is raging and the stakes are high. God has chosen spiritual leaders for the hour, and it is our responsibility to offer ourselves as willing vessels in whatever role God has chosen for us and to work in unity with the rest of the team. As the hour grows darker and the battle rages hotter, there should be a deeper resolve and more careful consideration within each of our hearts to make sure we are truly committed to God's plan and not just involved in some religious exercise.

Every Christian is looking forward to the end of the battle and the joy and excitement of the promised victory. Judges 5 describes the scene of victory celebration that flowed from the hearts of Deborah and Barak. But this will be nothing comparable to the song of victory that will be sung by the countless multitudes standing around the great throne of God at the end of all our battles.

Victory will have been achieved only because God chose the right leaders for the right time. Those committed leaders invited others to become involved in God's great mission. Together God's people work hard, stay faithful, endure the necessary sacrifices, and will someday sing the song of redemption together.

17

5
week of
03.31.13

The Cautious Conqueror

Lesson Text

Judges 6:15, 36-40

15 And he said unto him, Oh my Lord, wherewith shall I save Israel? behold, my family is poor in Manasseh, and I am the least in my father's house.

. . . . .

36 And Gideon said unto God, If thou wilt save Israel by mine hand, as thou hast said,

37 Behold, I will put a fleece of wool in the floor; and if the dew be on the fleece only, and it be dry upon all the earth beside, then shall I know that thou wilt save Israel by mine hand, as thou hast said.

38 And it was so: for he rose up early on the morrow, and thrust the fleece together, and wringed the dew out of the fleece, a bowl full of water.

39 And Gideon said unto God, Let not thine anger be hot against me, and I will speak but this once: let me prove, I pray thee, but this once with the fleece; let it now be dry only upon the fleece, and upon all the ground let there be dew.

40 And God did so that night: for it was dry upon the fleece only, and there was dew on all the ground

Judges 7:19-22

19 So Gideon, and the hundred men that were with him, came unto the outside of the camp in the beginning of the middle watch; and they had but newly set the watch: and they blew the trumpets, and brake the pitchers that were in their hands.

20 And the three companies blew the trumpets, and brake the pitchers, and held the lamps in their left hands, and the trumpets in their right hands to blow withal: and they cried, The sword of the LORD, and of Gideon.

21 And they stood every man in his place round about the camp: and all the host ran, and cried, and fled.

22 And the three hundred blew the trumpets, and the LORD set every man's sword against his fellow, even throughout all the host: and the host fled to Beth-shittah in Zererath, and to the border of Abel-meholah, unto Tabbath.

Focus Thought

Both doing God's will and being certain of God's will are equally important.

Focus Verse

Philippians 4:13

I can do all things through Christ which strengtheneth me.

18

Live the Adventure

by Daniel J. Koren

In a world focused on entertainment, North Americans seem to lack the spirit of adventure that made us famous. Rather than risk anything, too many believers hide behind soft lives and safe livelihoods. Not so for church-builder Wayne Huntley.

Doing a great work for God as an evangelist and assistant pastor, Brother Huntley could have continued to do well for himself and his family without taking risks. Instead, he responded to the call of God to return to his native state and grow a work for God. No, an angel did not find him hiding from the enemy, but he did have a divine visitation that let him know Raleigh needed a hero.

Elected as pastor by five members in a suburb of Raleigh, the Huntley family lived for a time in a 22-foot travel trailer parked beside the church. He taught Bible studies, led attendance drives, and visited the local hospital to reach out to those in need. Slowly, momentum grew.

Over the years, God has blessed his efforts among those who do not know the truth. Today, the Temple of Pentecost is an outreach and revival center. What began as something humble and unnoticed became great because someone was willing to come out of hiding and stand up against the enemy.

Hundreds of cities both urban and rural scream for a Gideon to lead them. Church planters are mighty men and women of valor. How could you team up with others or support someone to reach a community nearby?

Contemplating the Topic

Both doing God's will and being certain of God's will are equally important. There is danger in not knowing the will of God, but an even greater risk comes with knowing God's will but failing to follow it through to completion. For the believer, it is imperative first to discover God's purpose, and then to align our will and actions with His divine plan.

Searching the Scriptures

I. GOD'S PLAN UNFOLDS

When Deborah and Barak passed from the scene and Israel lapsed back into idolatry, God sent the next "spoilers," a loose-jointed collection of Midianites, Amalekites, and Eastern peoples. For seven years this motley assortment of raiders plundered and slaughtered in Israel, leaving the people of God impoverished, starving, and hiding in caves. They finally cried out to God for deliverance, but this time God listened reluctantly. While His people sent up pleas to Him for deliverance, their hearts still belonged to Baal. The suc-cessive chastisements designed to turn the people's hearts toward Him seemed to have no lasting effect. Divine jealously burned hot.

A. The Messenger Arrives

For the first time since Othniel, rather than sending a judge God sent a prophet with a message: God alone had delivered His people from Egypt and given them the Land of Promise; therefore He demanded and deserved their faithful love and allegiance. (See Judges 6:8-10.) They began to realize God would not answer their pleas until they heeded this message.

B. Gideon Arrives

After sending the prophet to the people, God sent an angelic messenger to a humble Manassehite threshing his wheat behind the winepress in an attempt to hide his crop from the enemy. The angel proclaimed, "The LORD is with thee, thou mighty man of valour" (Judges 6:12). Although Gideon's name means "Destroyer," "Mighty warrior," or "Feller (of trees)," at the time of the angelic visitation Gideon was no great warrior. He was the youngest member of the poorest family in the smallest tribe of Israel.

God saw character and spiritual traits in Gideon that caused Him to choose the man as a judge for this critical time. Gideon's immediate response to the angel's message revealed a love for Israel, ability to listen to the voice of God, and willingness to follow in trust and faith. That same night Gideon threw down the altar of Baal and fueled a sacrifice with the "wood of the grove" (Judges 6:25-26).

C. The Message Is Delivered

The message of God not only spoke deliverance to the people from their current crisis, but recognized the larger problem that existed. During the seven years without godly leadership, Israel had strayed from God's protective hand and into the enemy's hands. They crawled into earthen holes and rocky caves for protection and shelter.

People and nations will frequently wander away from God by rebelling against His Word and then question where He is in their time of trouble. When natural disasters or enemy attacks come, they are left without divine defense. It is important to note, however, that these external enemies cannot destroy the people of God; the real destroyers are unbelief and spiritual degeneration within their own hearts.

II. GIDEON IS CAUTIOUS

A. Gideon Questions the Angel

Gideon was not a warrior or a great military commander. Instead, he was a farmer who was hiding his wheat crop from the Midianites. Gideon had not been groomed to take command of an army; he had no knowledge of military tactics, no training in the use of weaponry, and no ability to lead soldiers into battle. He had always led a simple life, existing from day to day. His thoughts, time, and energy had been devoted to taking care of his family and surviving enemy raids. It probably had never occurred to him that he could serve the nation as a leader of the same caliber as Deborah.

B. God Responds

Gideon's first concern was his perceived lack of ability to do what God was asking. Gideon said, "Oh my Lord, wherewith shall I save Israel?" (Judges 6:15). Both Moses at the burning bush and Jeremiah encountered this same challenge. (See Exodus 3:11; Jeremiah 1:6.) God ignored their objections with the declaration that He would tell them what to say,

strengthen them for the task, and enable them to accomplish it. Similarly, God responded to Gideon, "Surely I will be with thee, and thou shalt smite the Midianites as one man" (Judges 6:16). It is clear God wanted both Gideon and the people to recognize His divine power working among them to bring deliverance.

C. The Fleece

Gideon's words testify to the fact that he knew he was taking a risk to use a fleece to confirm God's promise. "Testing" God was a violation of Jewish law. (The Hebrew word translated *tempt* in Deuteronomy 6:16 is the same word translated *test* here.) But Gideon needed assurance that he was, in fact, hearing from God, so he proposed a plan in which he would place a fleece of wool on the ground. The first night, the dew was to be on the fleece but not on the ground. The second night, the dew was to be upon the ground but not the fleece. On both occasions, God confirmed His Word.

D. The Enemy's Nightmare

The night before the planned attack, God told Gideon if he was still unsure to slip down to the outskirts of the enemy's camp and listen to what the soldiers were saying. He and his servant Phurah ventured near a tent and overheard a soldier talking to his companion.

Did the man speak with awe and fear, or with derision? Obviously, Midianite spies had infiltrated Israeli territory, for they knew of Gideon and the exploits of Israel's God. And they also had seen the extreme reduction of Gideon's army. It is possible they regarded Gideon's puny military force as threatening as a tumbling barley loaf. But Gideon knew how to interpret the dream. It assured him that Israel would win the victory over the Midianites, even though they were far outnumbered.

Today, the believer has the same assurance, for John wrote, "Ye are of God, little children, and have overcome them [spirits of antichrists]: because greater is he that is in you, than he that is in the world" (I John 4:4). Jesus said, "In the world ye shall have tribulation: but be of good cheer; I have overcome the world" (John 16:33).

III. CAUTION TURNS TO COURAGE

A. Call to Service

Moved by the Spirit of God, Gideon sounded a trumpet and sent messengers to his own tribe of Manasseh and the tribes to the north, calling them to battle. Thirty-two thousand warriors answered the call and assembled in Harod on Manasseh's northern border, not far from the enemy camp.

God said, "The people that are with thee are too many for me to give the Midianites into their hands, lest Israel vaunt themselves against me, saying, Mine own hand hath saved me" (Judges 7:2). God wanted credit for the victory and would win it with only a handful of the bold and the brave. "Tell the ones who are afraid to go back home." Twenty-two thousand turned back. They were afraid to take the risk of stepping over the line from defensive mode into offensive mode.

Of the ten thousand remaining men, God reduced the number to just three hundred men. Within hours, the Israelite army had shrunk by 94 percent.

Because it sometimes is hard for us to understand God's instructions, we often expect Him to accept our idea of the best way to approach the problem, instead of seeking His plan.

B. The Response

Gideon's orders were simple but crucial. No one was to make a move without his direct order. Their success depended upon obedience to God's commands to Gideon and relied upon the element of surprise. Our victory in working for the Lord also depends upon complete obedience to God's plan.

Gideon divided his men into three companies, and they crept down the hillside in the dark of night until they were just above the slumbering enemy camp. Then pitchers crashed, lights blazed, shouts rang out, and trumpets blared. Disoriented, confused, and terrified, the enemy force made up of various Bedouins could not distinguish between friend or foe. Some turned on one another with their swords while others turned to flee in fear. Gideon's men took off after them; and when the Israelite warriors who had gone home realized victory was imminent, they joined the fray.

C. Courage Keeps Marching

Israel chased the Bedouins to the borders of their tribal lands. With the Midianites in retreat, Gideon easily could have returned home, but he did not.

With momentum flowing, there was no time to rest. He wanted to gain every advantage possible from the victory. If he did not

destroy the kings of Midian, they would rally and return to harass Israel as before. It was time to secure the land for the future, and then they could celebrate.

Gideon and his three hundred men pursued the Bedouins across the fords of the Jordan River and deep into the desert, again surprising them by ambushing them in their own territory. He dispatched the Midianite kings and princes. Only 15,000 warriors of the people of the East remained, out of a force of 135,000. Gideon attributed the victory to God.

D. Ultimate Victory

At the conclusion of the battle, the people pleaded with Gideon to become their ruler. Although he served as their judge and oversaw forty years of peace, he recognized that the Lord had brought deliverance. Peace would continue only when they submitted to His divine authority and worshiped Him alone.

Internalizing the Message

We can glean several lessons from the story of Gideon.

1. When we allow our loyalties to stray and our dedication to waver, God sometimes sends affliction to draw our focus back to Him.

Both the Hebrew and the Greek words for *chasten* mean to correct, reprove, instruct, discipline, even smite. When the affliction causes us to turn back to Him, we call for help and He will hear. (See Psalm 106.)

2. God will hear us, but He will not send deliverance before sending His Word. He wants us to repent and restore our covenant relationship with Him. Then He will send deliverance. We may not understand the reason for the instructions He gives, but if we obey His Word and do not try to win the victory in our own way, deliverance will come. (See Acts 3:19).

3. God chose Gideon, one of the most unlikely men in the country, to deliver His people from the Midianites. God still delights in choosing unlikely candidates to accomplish His will.

4. So many foes and obstacles stand in the way that achieving victory seems impossible. Just as God reduced Gideon's fighting force to three hundred men so no one could claim personal credit for the victory, when victory comes to us we cannot claim it for ourselves; victory belongs to God.

6
week of
04.07.13

Restoration of the Rebel

Lesson Text

Judges 16:4-5, 13, 16, 20-21, 28-30

4 And it came to pass afterward, that he loved a woman in the valley of Sorek, whose name was Delilah.

5 And the lords of the Philistines came up unto her, and said unto her, Entice him, and see wherein his great strength lieth, and by what means we may prevail against him, that we may bind him to afflict him: and we will give thee every one of us eleven hundred pieces of silver.

. . . . .

13 And Delilah said unto Samson, Hitherto thou hast mocked me, and told me lies: tell me wherewith thou mightest be bound. And he said unto her, If thou weavest the seven locks of my head with the web.

. . . . .

16 And it came to pass, when she pressed him daily with her words, and urged him, so that his soul was vexed unto death;

. . . . .

20 And she said, The Philistines be upon thee, Samson. And he awoke out of his sleep, and said, I will go out as at other times before, and shake myself. And he wist not that the LORD was departed from him.

21 But the Philistines took him, and put out his eyes, and brought him down to Gaza, and bound him with fetters of brass; and he did grind in the prison house.

. . . . .

28 And Samson called unto the LORD, and said, O Lord GOD, remember me, I pray thee, and strengthen me, I pray thee, only this once, O God, that I may be at once avenged of the Philistines for my two eyes.

29 And Samson took hold of the two middle pillars upon which the house stood, and on which it was borne up, of the one with his right hand, and of the other with his left.

30 And Samson said, Let me die with the Philistines. And he bowed himself with all his might; and the house fell upon the lords, and upon all the people that were therein. So the dead which he slew at his death were more than they which he slew in his life.

Focus Thought

God's mercy extends to those who through careless acts choose the path of the foolish.

Focus Verse

Galatians 6:1

Brethren, if a man be overtaken in a fault, ye which are spiritual, restore such an one in the spirit of meekness; considering thyself, lest thou also be tempted.

Restore the Fallen
by Daniel J. Koren

A pastor we will call Sam fell into sin. His moment of weakness hurt his wife and family, who worked with him through his repentance and forgave him. After moving away from the community where he had suffered a tarnished reputation, he determined to live for God. Within a short time, the call of God stirred him to reach the lost again. He began bringing people to the church in the town where he now lived, baptizing them in Jesus' name, and seeing the Spirit fill them. In a few years he won dozens to the Lord.

He accepted his pastor's gracious invitation to serve as the church's staff evangelist. Over the years hundreds of souls have been added to the Kingdom by his tireless desire to teach Bible studies and do outreach. One day, a visitor who knew Sam's dishonorable past remarked, "How could your pastor have *him* as a staff member?" Once told of the minister's devotion to the Lord and his labors in the harvest, the voice of the accuser had nothing more to say. Perhaps we would have a stronger army if we shot fewer of our wounded and helped them get back into the fight instead.

Jesus said His mission was to bring back the straying sheep. One He restored was Peter. How many heroes could come back if we let them? Sam got a grip on his purpose again and is still tearing down strongholds.

Contemplating the Topic

God chose Samson "to deliver Israel out of the hand of the Philistines" after forty years of oppression. He deliberately broke his Nazarite vows, committed fornication with a harlot, and trifled with the spiritual power the Almighty had given him. How could the Lord be so patient and gracious? How could a holy God restore such a seemingly unholy rebel?

Searching the Scriptures

I. THE CARELESS STRONG MAN

A. Blessed Beginning

The future deliverer of Israel was to be no ordinary child, for the angel of the Lord charged Samson's mother not to partake of strong drink or eat anything unclean; thus, Samson was to be a Nazarite while still in his mother's womb, not from any vow he took later. How carefully Manoah and his wife must have instructed their son as it became more and more evident God was with him. As Samson grew, "the Spirit of the LORD began to move him at times in the camp of Dan" (Judges 13:25).

B. Blurred Goals

On one of Samson's forays across the border between Dan and Philistia he "saw a woman in Timnath of the daughters of the Philistines" (Judges 14:1) whom he immediately wanted to marry. The law of God forbade such a union, and Samson's parents asked, "Is there never a woman among the daughters of thy brethren, or among all my people, that thou goest to take a wife of the uncircumcised Philistines?" (Judges 14:3). But reckless desire prevailed over godly reason. "And Samson said unto his father, Get her for me; for she pleaseth me well" (Judges 14:3).

C. Selfish Carnality

Samson's attitude and actions reveal he relegated God's plan and purpose to the backseat while he sought immediate gratification, thinking the Lord would strengthen him always. He slew a thousand Philistine warriors with the jawbone of an ass, then grumbled to the Lord that he was dying of thirst. At Gaza he visited a harlot and the same night walked away with the city gates on his shoulders.

II. SOREK'S TRAGIC LOVE AFFAIR

A. Fatal Attraction

Delilah's physical charms lured Samson away from whatever moral values he still held. Far from being delicate or dainty as her name implied, Delilah was a conniving prostitute who, as the proverbial woman in Proverbs 6:26, hunted for "the precious life" in order to destroy it. Foolishly, Samson must have believed she returned his love; yet, his ardor did not totally blind him to reality. He knew

Delilah was not the type of woman with whom his parents would arrange his marriage.

B. Enemy's Plan

The lords of the five major Philistine cities (see Joshua 13:3; I Samuel 6:17; Judges 3:3) agreed that Samson must be stopped. If ropes could not hold him, if weapons of war could not conquer him, then perhaps the wiles of a seductive woman such as Delilah could overcome him.

C. Vow Violated

Delilah nagged until Samson said, "There hath not come a razor upon mine head; for I have been a Nazarite unto God from my mother's womb: if I be shaven, then my strength will go from me" (Judges 16:17). Delighted, the temptress petted him until she lulled him to sleep on her knee. She sent for the lords of the Philistines who came immediately and poured silver into her hands. Then she sent for a man who shaved Samson's head.

III. SIN'S VICTORY

A. Loss of Strength

When Delilah cried, "The Philistines be upon thee!" Samson awoke out of sleep and thought, *I'll go out as at other times before, and shake myself.* But it would be not be "as at other times before."

The Hebrew champion did not realize until it was too late that Delilah had shaved his head while he lay asleep and helpless. "He wist not that the LORD was departed from him" (Judges 16:20).

B. Loss of Freedom

As the people of the Lord, we are meant to rejoice in our freedom. We have an enemy who is determined to bind us by whatever means. But we can draw nigh to God, resist the devil, and cause him to flee. "Where the Spirit of the Lord is, there is liberty" (II Corinthians 3:17).

C. Loss of Vision

We can only imagine the suffering Samson must have endured at the hands of the Philistines. They put out his eyes (literally, "bored them out").

IV. GOD'S MERCY

A. Struggle for Restoration

If a person falters in his commitment to God, the Lord can bring him back to a place of service. If he experiences moral failure, God can grant repentance and remove the scales from his eyes. If temptation overtakes him, a fellow believer can be instrumental in re-establishing him on solid footing. (See Galatians 6:1.)

B. Strength Returns

Along with the renewal of his vows, it seems Samson's strength began to return. He sensed the nearness of God and felt a divine stirring within his heart. Could it be the Spirit of God was actually moving upon him again? Was it possible the same divine power he had once felt was being restored to him after he had failed so miserably?

C. Final Victory

When the Philistine's "hearts were merry" (Judges 16:25)—no doubt with wine, as in Judges 9:27—they called for Samson to be led out of prison to the temple. They made sport of him as a dirty, blind, clumsy buffoon. Amid the tumult of the crowd Samson cried to God. "O Lord GOD, remember me, I pray thee, and strengthen me, I pray thee, only this once" (Judges 16:28). God remembered, for He had never really forgotten. The dead which Samson "slew at his death were more than they which he slew in his life" (Judges 16:30).

Internalizing the Message

As believers, we have been called to a life of separation. When we were born again our Father endued us with power from on high. Like Samson, God chose us as His peculiar treasure. We must keep the temple of our bodies clean and holy that we may honor the Lord Jesus Christ and maintain a spiritual relationship with Him. We must continue in communion with the abiding presence of God. If we allow temptation to overtake us and defile our minds and bodies with worldly pleasures, God will withdraw His presence, blessing, and anointing from our lives. The very things that tempted us will enslave us.

But thank the Lord, He is not willing that any should perish. His mercy keeps the way to repentance open; He longs and waits to reconcile us and restore us. He "is longsuffering to us-ward, not willing that any should perish, but that all should come to repentance" (II Peter 3:9).

Wealth of Wise Choices

7

Lesson Text

I Kings 3:7-13

7 And now, O LORD my God, thou hast made thy servant king instead of David my father: and I am but a little child: I know not how to go out or come in.

8 And thy servant is in the midst of thy people which thou hast chosen, a great people, that cannot be numbered nor counted for multitude.

9 Give therefore thy servant an understanding heart to judge thy people, that I may discern between good and bad: for who is able to judge this thy so great a people?

10 And the speech pleased the Lord, that Solomon had asked this thing.

11 And God said unto him, Because thou hast asked this thing, and hast not asked for thyself long life; neither hast asked riches for thyself, nor hast asked the life of thine enemies; but hast asked for thyself understanding to discern judgment;

12 Behold, I have done according to thy words: lo, I have given thee a wise and an understanding heart; so that there was none like thee before thee, neither after thee shall any arise like unto thee.

13 And I have also given thee that which thou hast not asked, both riches, and honour: so that there shall not be any among the kings like unto thee all thy days.

I Kings 12:6-8

6 And king Rehoboam consulted with the old men, that stood before Solomon his father while he yet lived, and said, How do ye advise that I may answer this people?

7 And they spake unto him, saying, If thou wilt be a servant unto this people this day, and wilt serve them, and answer them, and speak good words to them, then they will be thy servants for ever.

8 But he forsook the counsel of the old men, which they had given him, and consulted with the young men that were grown up with him, and which stood before him.

Focus Thought

Right choices bring blessings.

Focus Verse

Proverbs 9:1

Wisdom hath builded her house, she hath hewn out her seven pillars.

He That Winneth Souls
by Daniel J. Koren

Today, young men and women still make the wise request of Solomon. Rather than pursuing money or popular culture, they humble themselves to lay hold of that which is most valuable. The wisest among us lay hold on a lifestyle of winning souls and helping start churches.

In his book *The Wisdom and Power of the Cross*, J. T. Pugh told of Richard Eastman and his wife pioneering a work in Montana. He said they had "only fifty-two dollars, and no job. Neither did they have cooking utensils nor other needs of life. But pot pies could be purchased at five for a dollar. Since they had nothing to cook with, they went into the national forest nearby and cooked on an open fire."

While such a lifestyle is not applauded in our convenience-oriented culture, such sacrifices have brought the gospel to millions. We need more people of wisdom like Richard Eastman to plant churches and children who love the Lord. His son and daughter have gone on to participate in the ministry as well.

Our nation needs men and women of wisdom to rescue its people. When parents train up children in wisdom as Solomon's parents did, we prepare them to rescue the perishing among us. (See Proverbs 4:3-4.) Many religious groups acclimate their children to think of nothing else but growing up to do outreach work and missions trips. Too many Apostolic homes shape children who live only for more gadgets, possessions, and friends. What might we become as a movement if we tailored our homes toward the wisdom of church planting?

Contemplating the Topic

We often face overwhelming situations in life. The challenge looks too great. The mountain looks too high. The mission field seems too big. Situations like this require wisdom. We need to know how to acquire it and what it is. Young Solomon may not have known what wisdom was, but he knew where to get it. Regardless of our opportunities or challenges, we can all go to the same source of wisdom.

Searching the Scriptures

I. SOLOMON'S WISE CHOICE

A. Chose Wisdom Instead of Alternatives

Solomon could have asked for world renown, riches, superpower, or long life. Instead, he asked for wisdom—something that would benefit everyone, not just himself.

B. Received God's Added Blessings

Solomon's wise choice pleased God, and He gave Solomon not only wisdom, but also unprecedented riches and honor.

II. REHOBOAM'S FOOLISH CHOICE

Unfortunately, Solomon did not pass his wisdom on to his son Rehoboam, even though he addressed many of the proverbs to his son. Rehoboam grew up in luxury but overlooked what gave his father such success. Perhaps he never read his father's proverbs. Some young people tend to discard the Golden Rule to chase after the chrome and sparkle of this decaying world.

A. Consulted Elders

When the elders approached Rehoboam with the need to lower the burden apparently of excessive taxes being collected from the people, the new king mulled over his response.

B. Consulted His Peers

Rehoboam consulted his peers. Like a person asking what is ahead from someone who cannot see beyond the end of his nose, the new king asked for long-term direction from those without perspective or experience. These peers shared his misguided values; luxury and indulgence had skewed their thinking. They wanted more money as much as Rehoboam wanted it. They advised him to increase the burdens of the people higher than ever before. And he did.

C. Made Decision of Doom

In the end Rehoboam's lust for more left him with less. Ten tribes seceded from his kingdom, leaving only Judah and Benjamin.

Wisdom has perspective. It has a vision of the end result of each action. Foolishness thinks only of the immediate goal. Foolishness is the donkey gobbling up the oats from the trough, not knowing where the next scoop will come from. Wisdom is the farmer plowing a field, sowing, harvesting, and storing up grain for many years to come. (See Proverbs 10:4-5; 12:11.)

III. MAKING RIGHT CHOICES

A. Choices Are Personal but Affect Others

Do we view the world with the perspective, "There's not enough to go around," or "There'll always be enough for everybody"? If we know God is the source of all good things, we will never feel disadvantaged. If we feel we must make our own way in life, we will always grasp at the last bit of "gold dust" in a desperate bid for significance.

Whether we make wise or foolish choices affects many more than ourselves. Foolish drivers injure and kill many more than just themselves. Foolish parents make their children suffer.

B. Wisdom Makes Systematic Right Choices

A wise life operates on at least seven essential pillars of prudence: financial management, organization, preventative healthcare, time management, education, proper relationships, and spiritual disciplines. We will consider each of these in turn. While most believers will find some of these principles already at work in their lives, we all have to put effort into a few.

Finance Management. A wise person is not cheap, but careful. Cheapness cheats. The cheap farmer may feed sawdust instead of oats, thinking he has fooled the horse—until it falls over dead. Rather than shortchange ourselves with buying the cheapest item on the shelf, we should invest in good, durable items. The art of bargain hunting bypasses the see-and-grab spending that puts people in the poorhouse.

One cannot be wiser with money than to give generously. (See Proverbs 3:9-10.) A wise steward not only gives tithes to the local church for the support of the ministry, but also gives an additional amount to help provide for the upkeep and advancement of the church.

Organization. Wise people control their environment. Clutter is an expensive management system; when you cannot find an item, you have to buy another. On the floor, it gets broken or soiled. Many people would not be late for church if they put things away (children's shoes, special outfits, and other necessities). Teaching children to organize while they are young saves them many headaches later in life.

Preventative Health. "Hast thou found honey? eat so much as is sufficient for thee, lest thou be filled therewith, and vomit it" (Proverbs 25:16). On the whole, North America has a weight and nutrition problem. If we can prevent the problem by managing our eating and exercise properly, we are being far better stewards.

Schedule. If a person fails to plan, he simply plans to fail. The all-wise God wants us to "number our days, that we may apply our hearts unto wisdom" (Psalm 90:12). Wisdom takes stock of the day and makes the most of it. We shape our destiny by the hour. The Book of Job introduces us to the wisdom literature in the Old Testament. Job lived in the discipline of rising early in the morning to call on the name of the Lord. No schedule or calendar will stand if God does not come first in it.

Education. "Wise men lay up knowledge" (Proverbs 10:14). We should continually grow mentally and intellectually.

Proper Relationships. The Golden Rule gives proper spacing and alignment to the other pillars of wisdom. If we have wrong perceptions about our interaction with other people, they will skew the other disciplines.

Spiritual Discipline. A person can have all of the above qualities, but not to have this last pillar is to weaken and eventually implode the whole building of wisdom.

Internalizing the Message

Wisdom knows "the wages of sin is death" (Romans 6:23) and therefore makes provision for making systematic, wise choices in the little things so that big choices are no big deal. Fortunately we do not rely on just learned wisdom and practical advice, for we speak "not the wisdom of this world, nor of the princes of this world, . . . but we speak the wisdom of God in a mystery" pertaining to things the eye cannot perceive nor the mind learn, "even the hidden wisdom," which the natural man cannot discern, but "God hath revealed them unto us by his Spirit: for the Spirit searcheth all things, yea, the deep things of God" (I Corinthians 2:6-7, 10).

8

Integrity Takes a Stand

Lesson Text

I Kings 15:9-15, 22-24

9 And in the twentieth year of Jeroboam king of Israel reigned Asa over Judah.

10 And forty and one years reigned he in Jerusalem. And his mother's name was Maachah, the daughter of Abishalom.

11 And Asa did that which was right in the eyes of the LORD, as did David his father.

12 And he took away the sodomites out of the land, and removed all the idols that his fathers had made.

13 And also Maachah his mother, even her he removed from being queen, because she had made an idol in a grove; and Asa destroyed her idol, and burnt it by the brook Kidron.

14 But the high places were not removed: nevertheless Asa's heart was perfect with the LORD all his days.

15 And he brought in the things which his father had dedicated, and the things which himself had dedicated, into the house of the LORD, silver, and gold, and vessels.

. . . . .

22 Then king Asa made a proclamation throughout all Judah; none was exempted: and they took away the stones of Ramah, and the timber thereof, wherewith Baasha had builded; and king Asa built with them Geba of Benjamin, and Mizpah.

23 The rest of all the acts of Asa, and all his might, and all that he did, and the cities which he built, are they not written in the book of the chronicles of the kings of Judah? Nevertheless in the time of his old age he was diseased in his feet.

24 And Asa slept with his fathers, and was buried with his fathers in the city of David his father: and Jehoshaphat his son reigned in his stead.

Focus Thought

Integrity gives one the courage to do right.

Focus Verse

Philippians 2:12

Wherefore, my beloved, as ye have always obeyed, not as in my presence only, but now much more in my absence, work out your own salvation with fear and trembling.

Doing What's Right
by Richard M. Davis

Dr. Peter J. Sireno, president of Darton College in Albany, Georgia, wrote the following to the college family: "One of the most critical challenges our College faces in maintaining our success is preventing losses caused by unethical, illegal, or unsafe acts. Each of us shares the responsibility for meeting this challenge.

"Fortunately, the most effective way to maintain an ethical, honest College is captured in the phrase, 'doing what's right.' 'Doing what's right' brings out the best in you, your co-workers, and your school, and that is why we are pleased to introduce the Doing What's Right program."

I have no knowledge about Darton College, its faculty, or its mission. I neither endorse the institution nor advise against it. However, I was impressed by this communication to the faculty and staff. The theme of Dr. Sireno's letter was to do what's right.

To do the right thing would solve many problems in life. If individuals would follow their hearts and abide by the unchanging principles of right instead of wrong, lawful instead of unlawful, and appropriate instead of inappropriate, they would avoid many heartaches and troubles. Further, they should avoid the extreme edges of these considerations. Too many people in this post-modern age live life on the edge—trying just to get by. They are complacent to do what is legal, but questionable; acceptable, but inadvisable; possible, but unethical.

As reiterated by the Focus Thought for our lesson today, integrity gives a person the courage to do what's right. We need individuals of integrity to lead in our world today.

As enunciated by Paul the apostle, "All things are lawful for me, but all things are not expedient: all things are lawful for me, but all things edify not" (I Corinthians 10:23).

Contemplating the Topic

Today's lesson focuses on Asa, the third king of Judah, God's answer to the desperate plight of a nation wallowing in the mire of apostasy. Idolatry and perversion had a stranglehold on Judah during the reigns of Rehoboam, Solomon's son, and Abijam, Rehoboam's son. (See I Kings 14:22-24; 15:3.) These two men were products of the idolatry insinuated into the national culture by Solomon's fascination with the false gods of his many heathen wives. The only reason God preserved the line of the kings of Judah was His love for David and the promises He had made to him. (See I Kings 15:4; II Samuel 7.)

Searching the Scriptures

I. ASA'S BACKGROUND

Approximately sixty years of leadership by Solomon, Rehoboam, and Abijam handed a national disgrace to the new king, Asa, son of Abijam. Out of the wicked family background, doctrinal debris, and spiritual and social calamity arose a man with a heart for God—Asa.

A. Ungodly Parents

The Lord desires that parents train up "godly seed" unto the Lord. (See Malachi 2:11-16.) Asa did not have the advantage of godly parents. His father, Abijam, enjoyed the sinful practices of his father, Rehoboam, and saw no reason to hide his indulgences from his son, his nation, or his Lord. He presumed upon the love and favor God had bestowed upon his great-grandfather David, and the promise that David's royal line would endure forever. (See I Kings 15:4-5.)

There is no mention of Asa's mother. His grandmother, Maachah (I Kings 15:10, NKJV), was the favorite of Rehoboam's eighteen wives and the woman who apparently raised Asa. Maachah served Asherah, the mother goddess who in Bible times was associated with Baal, the god of fertility. Asherah's symbol was the sacred tree or pole, which corresponded to the stone pillar used in the Baal cult worship. (See Judges 6:28.)

B. No Wholesome Example

His nurturers were a sinful father and a scheming, self-willed grandmother who wanted to squash the young Asa under her thumb while she promoted worship of Asherah and Baal.

C. Worldly Environment

In some respects, Asa's home environment would match many of the homes in our generation, even in Pentecostal circles. The homes of some parents who claim a "born-again" experience are filled with worldliness. Multitudes in the Christian community want a Christ without a cross. They want a Pentecostal experience without a Calvary. They want the Spirit without a genuine experience in repentance.

II. ASA'S REIGN

A. Followed David's Example

What a remarkable testimony the Scriptures give concerning Asa! It does not state that Asa followed in the footsteps of his father, Abijam, but rather in the footsteps of "his father David," the man after God's own heart.

The Bible records David's sins as well as his righteous acts. Similarly, Asa's record contains blemishes. When Baasha, king of Israel, invaded Judah and began to fortify militarily the city of Ramah, only five miles north of Jerusalem, Asa became worried. Baasha blocked traffic going either way on the main roads, cutting off their trade. Instead of seeking God's help as he did when Zera the Ethiopian threatened him from the south, Asa took treasures from the Temple and sent them to the king of Syria, asking him to oust Baasha from Judean territory. Baasha retreated as soon as the treaty was formed. This did not go unnoticed by God. He sent the prophet Hanani to rebuke Asa for his association with an ungodly king.

We as Christians contend with our flesh every day. We never will achieve perfection fully while we are still in this body. Therefore, how can God claim our hearts are perfect as he declared for David and Asa when we all have committed sin? Thank God He sees us not as flawed, unusable individuals but as individuals who are perfect or complete in Him—valuable, useful vessels in His kingdom. When we repent, He forgives and refuses even to remember our wrongdoing.

B. Removed Idols

In the fourteenth year of Asa's reign, a mighty Ethiopian army marched against Judah with one million men and three hundred chariots. (See II Chronicles 14:9.) Asa cried out to the Lord for help and the Lord smote the Ethiopians until they fled. Asa and his men gathered up "much spoil" (II Chronicles 14:13) and returned to Jerusalem. The

prophet Azariah met Asa on the way and preached a message.

Asa had given his heart to God at a young age, but now, emboldened by Azariah's message, he took courage to spark a revival in the entire nation. To do this he would have to throw off the dominance of his grandmother and undo the damage to the kingdom she and her son Abijam had caused.

Even without wooden idols, we are guilty of idolatry if we put anything in our lives above God. In this materialistic society, many people claim to know God but are wrapped up in the pursuit of making money and acquiring things. But the Bible says, "The love of money is the root of all evil: which while some coveted after, they have erred from the faith, and pierced themselves through with many sorrows" (I Timothy 6:10). Some of these individuals may covet money so passionately they are unfaithful to the house of the Lord, or they do not pay tithes or give in offerings according to the Scriptures. They neglect prayer and other essential disciplines for living life by the Holy Spirit. Covetousness fills their heart with idolatry. Let us reject all idolatry, whatever kind it may be.

Not only did Asa destroy the worship of idols, but he also banished the Sodomites from the land and suppressed the brothels. The ministry and the laity of our day must have the courage and the integrity to stand up against the onslaught of those who aggressively pursue and advance their ungodly and perverted lifestyles, striving to win their "rights" in the courts and impose their agenda on the rest of society. Christians must neither accept nor condone their perverse and abominable lifestyles.

God hates sin—every kind of sin. We must not be guilty of condoning and sanctioning that which the Lord hates and condemns.

C. Favored of God

After Asa cleansed the land, he led the people in a renewal of the covenant with God, which had not been done since the days of David. Asa first restored the altar of the Lord (II Chronicles 15:8). Then he sent invitations throughout Judah and Benjamin and "those who dwelt with them" (II Chronicles 15:9, NKJV) to assemble for the covenant renewal. The people of Ephraim, Manasseh, and Simeon flocked to Jerusalem and "entered into a covenant to seek the LORD God of their fathers with all their heart and with all their soul" (II Chronicles 15:12).

There is a lesson here for churches today. We must never do away with or abandon our prayer rooms. Hype, sensationalism, and drama can never substitute for genuine communication with the Almighty. We must continue to pray and seek God in repentance, asking Him for a continuing pouring out of His Holy Spirit in our day.

III. ASA'S STAND

A. Removed His Grandmother, the Queen

Dethroning the queen mother was a drastic step in the Near East, for the matriarchal position demanded great respect. But Maachah was the root of the apostasy in Judah and young Asa determined to uproot her from her position and destroy every evil thing she had done.

Christians should resist the temptation of condoning and approving wrongdoing among family members because of emotional ties or for fear of what they will say or do. We as Christians may not approve of what our family members or peers are doing, but if we stand passively by, ignoring the inner voice within us, we only contribute to the problem.

We should show appropriate respect without compromise. We have a responsibility to stand for what is right. We need to take courage, as Asa did, and refuse to be intimidated regardless of the person's position in the family. We should maintain our integrity and take a stand for right. We can confront the wrong by being tactful and firm rather than belligerent or dogmatic.

B. Walked Lonely Road of Integrity

Early in his life Asa loved God, sought God, and trusted God. More than popularity among the people, more than the approbation of peers, more than the approval of elders, he wanted to please God. The spark of divine inspiration in his heart motivated him to take an unpopular and seldom-used path.

Many who take a stand because of integrity, principle, and ethics walk a lonely path. Quite often those who do take a stand are criticized, cajoled, and even ostracized. Christ's own people falsely accused Him, erroneously tried Him, and turned Him over to the Roman authorities for crucifixion. They hated His claims to deity and His stand for truth and integrity. He said to His disciples, "If the world hate you, ye know that it hated me before it hated you. If ye were of the world, the world would love his own; but because ye are not of the world, but I have chosen you out of the world, therefore the world hateth you" (John 15:18-19).

C. Made No Exceptions

As part of the covenant renewal, Asa declared that those who chose not to participate in the covenant or seek the Lord would be executed. (See II Chronicles 15:13.) There were no exceptions whether small or great, man or woman.

This declaration stemmed from the covenantal terms in the law of Moses. No matter the relationship—brother, son, daughter, wife, or friend—if the person urged someone to go and serve other gods, Moses wrote, "Thou shalt not consent unto him, nor hearken unto him; neither shall thine eye pity him, neither shalt thou spare, neither shalt thou conceal him: but thou shalt surely kill him." (See Deuteronomy 13:6-11.) Israelites who worshiped false gods would experience the same annihilation God had ordered for the Canaanites who worshiped Baal, Asherah, Molech, Chemosh, and other abominable deities. The prescription to righteousness seemed harsh, but God knew it was necessary to separate His people from the cancerous influences of evil.

Asa's position of integrity harmonized with what Jesus expects of His followers. "He that loveth father or mother more than me is not worthy of me: and he that loveth son or daughter more than me is not worthy of me. And he that taketh not his cross, and followeth after me, is not worthy of me" (Matthew 10:37-38). "He that is not with me is against me; and he that gathereth not with me scattereth abroad" (Matthew 12:30). There is no compromise and there are no exceptions.

Internalizing the Message

Asa was a man of integrity, conviction, and courage. His godly example influenced an entire nation.

It is time for a revival of integrity in our generation. It must begin with leadership. Fathers need to be men of integrity. Husbands need to set a good example before their wives. Parents and grandparents need to be good examples of integrity, ethics, and principle before their children and grandchildren. All who are in leadership, secular or spiritual, must manifest integrity in every situation.

9

week of
04.28.13

No Price Is Right

Lesson Text

I Kings 21:1-8, 13-14

1 And it came to pass after these things, that Naboth the Jezreelite had a vineyard, which was in Jezreel, hard by the palace of Ahab king of Samaria.

2 And Ahab spake unto Naboth, saying, Give me thy vineyard, that I may have it for a garden of herbs, because it is near unto my house: and I will give thee for it a better vineyard than it; or, if it seem good to thee, I will give thee the worth of it in money.

3 And Naboth said to Ahab, The LORD forbid it me, that I should give the inheritance of my fathers unto thee.

4 And Ahab came into his house heavy and displeased because of the word which Naboth the Jezreelite had spoken to him: for he had said, I will not give thee the inheritance of my fathers. And he laid him down upon his bed, and turned away his face, and would eat no bread.

5 But Jezebel his wife came to him, and said unto him, Why is thy spirit so sad, that thou eatest no bread?

6 And he said unto her, Because I spake unto Naboth the Jezreelite, and said unto him, Give me thy vineyard for money; or else, if it please thee, I will give thee another vineyard for it: and he answered, I will not give thee my vineyard.

7 And Jezebel his wife said unto him, Dost thou now govern the kingdom of Israel? arise, and eat bread, and let thine heart be merry: I will give thee the vineyard of Naboth the Jezreelite.

8 So she wrote letters in Ahab's name, and sealed them with his seal, and sent the letters unto the elders and to the nobles that were in his city, dwelling with Naboth.

. . . . .

13 And there came in two men, children of Belial, and sat before him: and the men of Belial witnessed against him, even against Naboth, in the presence of the people, saying, Naboth did blaspheme God and the king. Then they carried him forth out of the city, and stoned him with stones, that he died.

14 Then they sent to Jezebel, saying, Naboth is stoned, and is dead.

Focus Thought

Our spiritual heritage is not for sale at any price.

Focus Verse

Matthew 16:26

For what is a man profited, if he shall gain the whole world, and lose his own soul? or what shall a man give in exchange for his soul?

A Heritage Worth Keeping
by Richard M. Davis

Naboth had a vineyard, an inheritance passed to him from his ancestors. More than property possessing natural value, to Naboth it was a heritage—something of enduring significance and value. For that reason, he refused to sell the property to Ahab and Jezebel.

Leaving an inheritance for our children and successors is noteworthy and commendable, but how much more important it is that we leave a spiritual heritage, an inheritance worth more than money can purchase—a heritage worth keeping, at any cost.

Christian author Randy Alcorn wrote about leaving our children a lasting spiritual legacy. In an article titled "Parenting Teens: Leaving a Lasting Spiritual Heritage," Alcorn wrote, "It only takes money to leave an inheritance. It takes character and spiritual vitality, 'a long obedience in the same direction,' to leave a true heritage.

"What will your kids remember?

"Dad was too busy to help me, too busy to talk with Mom, too busy to volunteer for even the most basic ministry at church, so busy reading the newspaper that there was no time for the Bible, so busy buying new cars there was no money to give to missions? If that's true, my friend, no amount of money you leave can cover up the fact that you have left your family nothing of eternal value.

"My mother left me no money, but she left me a heritage that I thank God for every day" (http://www.epm.org, "Parenting Teens: Leaving a Lasting Spiritual Heritage," accessed February 27, 2012).

Some things in life are worth keeping, whatever the cost. May we receive from our ancestors and leave for our posterity a spiritual heritage far too valuable to sell! There is no price we can put on things of lasting spiritual value.

Contemplating the Topic

Perhaps it is well that there is so little information given in the Scriptures about Naboth the Jezreelite. His name is mentioned only a few times. (See I Kings 21; II Kings 9:21, 25-26.) He was just a common farmer, unpolished and unpretentious, but with a backbone of steel. In the spiritual battle it is often the undistinguished and the lowly who become the point men in God's attack upon the forces of evil.

Searching the Scriptures

I. NABOTH'S INHERITANCE

A. His Hebrew Heritage

1. *Provided by Covenant.* Possession of the land meant more than simply the harvesting of bountiful crops or the viewing of stunning scenery. The land was a gift from God promised to Abraham, Isaac, Jacob, and their descendents. Moreover, the Jews were granted this land "for ever" (Genesis 13:14-15).

2. *No Exceptions.* The Mosaic law was clear. "No land is to be sold in perpetuity, for the land is mine, and you are only guests of mine, passing wayfarers" (Leviticus 25:23, *The Moffattt Translation of the Bible*). (See also Numbers 36:7.)

3. *To Be Treasured.* A farmer who tills and plants the land with his own hands has a natural love for the land. But a farmer in Israel in the ninth century BC viewed his land not just as a piece of real estate, but as a gift from God.

B. How He Treated His Inheritance

Naboth saw the promises and provisions of God for himself and for his family. Ahab could build all the palaces he wanted, even on land that bordered Naboth's, but the farmer found comfort in knowing this lush vineyard was and always would be his by inheritance.

II. AHAB'S OFFER

A. Ahab Made an Offer

Ahab offered Naboth what he considered a fair deal. "I will give thee for it a better vineyard than it; or, if it seem good to thee, I wiⁱ give thee the worth of it in money" (I Kⁱ

21:2). From a natural point of view the offer may have looked like an opportunity, a chance to strike a bargain with the king that would lead to greater prosperity. But from a spiritual viewpoint it was all wrong.

B. Naboth Refused the Offer

The world is taken aback when it meets a person who takes a strong stand for godly principles. Conviction seldom stands on center stage before a cheering crowd, but on this day in this vineyard Naboth stood by his convictions. Naboth entered his home with confidence he had done what was right, but Ahab went home "heavy and displeased" (I Kings 21:4). He "laid him down upon his bed, . . . and would eat no bread" (I Kings 1:4).

Jezebel said to him, "Dost thou now govern the kingdom of Israel? arise and eat bread, and let thine heart be merry: I will give thee the vineyard of Naboth the Jezreelite" (I Kings 21:7).

Ahab never considered the heinousness of the crime. He had received what he wanted and he was satisfied. Jezebel told him to take possession of the vineyard immediately before Naboth's family could object or before the matter was investigated further. Ahab hurried next door and was entering his beautiful vineyard only to be confronted by Elijah the Tishbite. "Hast thou found me, O mine enemy?" Ahab asked.

Elijah countered, "I have found thee: because thou hast sold thyself to work evil in the sight of the LORD" (I Kings 21:20). "Hast thou killed, and also taken possession? . . . In the place where dogs licked the blood of Naboth shall dogs lick thy blood, even thine" (I Kings 21:19). Further, the Lord's judgment extended to every male descendant of Ahab, and to Jezebel, who would be eaten by dogs by the wall of Jezreel.

III. OUR ETERNAL INHERITANCE

A. The World Makes Its Appeal

The world system runs counter to all that is godly and decent. It is a way of thinking and acting that originates with the devil himself. In every age since the Day of Pentecost, he has tempted Christians to conform to this system; and those who do, lose their relationship with God. For this reason John warned, "Love not the world, neither the things that are in the world. If any man love the world, the love of the Father is not in him" (I John 2:15). Paul wrote, "Be not conformed to this world" (Romans 12:2).

B. What Is Your Price?

There is a popular saying that "every man has his price." Esau smelled the spicy pottage and sold his birthright for "one morsel of meat" (Hebrews 12:16). Judas sold his Savior for thirty pieces of silver, "the common price of the meanest slave" (Adam Clarke). For others the price may be popularity or fame, wealth or prestige. Some sell their morals for a single night of pleasure or for a little cash in hand.

C. What Is the Worth of a Soul?

The value of a human soul is too profound for us to comprehend. The thought that a person will spend eternity as an immortal being either in a lost condition or in a saved condition is simply staggering. No tragedy in this life can compare to the loss of a soul. With the future suffering of the cross weighing heavily upon His mind, Jesus asked His disciples some heart-searching questions: "For what is a man profited, if he shall gain the whole world, and lose his own soul? or what shall a man give in exchange for his soul?" (Matthew 16:26).

God places tremendous value upon a soul. He paid the highest price, invested His dearest possession, and offered the greatest sacrifice to redeem us from our sin.

D. Compromise Is Not an Option

We must have the courage to withstand that which is evil and hold firmly to that which is right. We must not compromise our message on the new birth, on the oneness of God, or on our standards of holiness. These truths are essential. They are too precious to be bartered away for the sake of finding middle ground with a religious world that is constantly changing. We are doing a great work, and we cannot come down to the level of others who preach and teach a weaker message.

Internalizing the Message

Far better to toil in a vineyard within the will of God than to live in a palace where wickedness prevails! Courageous Naboth refused the king's demand to give up his inheritance. Do we have the courage to say no to a world that promises alluring enticements if we will give up our inheritance? Will we succumb to the pressures of the day to compromise our faith, or will we "buy the truth, and sell it not" (Proverbs 23:23)?

God's Rules Rule

10

week of
05.05.13

Lesson Text

II Kings 5:1-3, 8-11, 13-14

1 Now Naaman, captain of the host of the king of Syria, was a great man with his master, and honourable, because by him the LORD had given deliverance unto Syria: he was also a mighty man in valour, but he was a leper.

2 And the Syrians had gone out by companies, and had brought away captive out of the land of Israel a little maid; and she waited on Naaman's wife.

3 And she said unto her mistress, Would God my lord were with the prophet that is in Samaria! for he would recover him of his leprosy.

. . . . .

8 And it was so, when Elisha the man of God had heard that the king of Israel had rent his clothes, that he sent to the king, saying, Wherefore hast thou rent thy clothes? let him come now to me, and he shall know that there is a prophet in Israel.

9 So Naaman came with his horses and with his chariot, and stood at the door of the house of Elisha.

10 And Elisha sent a messenger unto him, saying, Go and wash in Jordan seven times, and thy flesh shall come again to thee, and thou shalt be clean.

11 But Naaman was wroth, and went away, and said, Behold, I thought, He will surely come out to me, and stand, and call on the name of the LORD his God, and strike his hand over the place, and recover the leper.

. . . . .

13 And his servants came near, and spake unto him, and said, My father, if the prophet had bid thee do some great thing, wouldest thou not have done it? how much rather then, when he saith to thee, Wash, and be clean?

14 Then went he down, and dipped himself seven times in Jordan, according to the saying of the man of God: and his flesh came again like unto the flesh of a little child, and he was clean.

Focus Thought

To be successful in the game of life, we must play by God's rules.

Focus Verse

II Kings 5:13

And his servants came near, and spake unto him, and said, My father, if the prophet had bid thee do some great thing, wouldest thou not have done it? how much rather then, when he saith to thee, Wash, and be clean?

Not My Way, but God's Way

by Richard M. Davis

Many people well remember the song made famous by Frank Sinatra, "My Way." Rewritten by Paul Anka after he heard the song in France and had acquired the publishing rights in 1967, Sinatra recorded the song in late 1968 (Paul Anka, "With Paul Anka, 'Rock Swings,' Part Two," interviewed on *Fresh Air*, WHYY, August 10, 2005).

While the song has a fetching melody and an easy-to-listen-to smooth delivery, as only Sinatra could deliver, its message can be somewhat disturbing to a believer in Jesus Christ. According to *www.lyricsondemand.com*, the last three lines of the first verse state:

I've lived a life that's full
I traveled each and ev'ry highway
And more, much more than this, I did it my way

Certainly, God gives to believers full and satisfying lives, and He also gives them the freedom of choice, but for believers it is never about doing it "our way." It is all about doing it "His way"! I am not my own; I have been bought with a price—the precious blood of Jesus Christ, my Savior.

We live in an independent age in which people take great pride in doing things for themselves and are resistant to accepting advice or help from others. They want to "do it their way." However, it does not matter what I think about a matter or how I think things should be accomplished; it only matters what God instructs about it. I must follow His way, not my own.

Had Naaman refused to follow God's instructions explicitly, as delivered by the prophet, he would not have been healed. It was good he did it God's way, and it is good when we follow God's way and obey His instructions.

Contemplating the Topic

When Peter wrote of those who are disobedient, he used an antonym of the word that means "faith." This word sometimes is translated "unbelieving" (I Peter 2:8, *apietheo*). God equates disobedience with unbelief. Without faith it is impossible to please God (Hebrews 11:6). This means each of us must learn to respect God's authority over us by hearing His words and showing our belief through obedience to His commands. We must acknowledge that God's rules apply to every area of life.

Searching the Scriptures

Why did a Syrian military hero ask a prophet of Israel to heal him of leprosy? The answer lies in a short review of history between the two countries.

During the reign of Ahab, Syria attacked Samaria twice but Israel routed them with the help of the Lord, not because they were in a right relationship with God, but because Syria had ridiculed God (I Kings 20:28). After the victory, Ahab formed a pact with Ben-hadad, king of Syria (I Kings 20:34), which greatly displeased the Lord. Three years later Ahab formed an alliance with Judah in order to take back the territory of Ramoth-Gilead from the Syrians. The Lord gave Syria the victory and Ahab was fatally wounded. Syria's domination over Israel at this time in history set the stage for the story of Naaman during the reign of Joram, Ahab's son.

I. THE WELL KNOWN

Many spiritual lessons can be derived from Old Testament stories. (For example, see Romans 15:4; I Corinthians 10:11.) Perhaps the story that teaches most vividly about the power and blessing that come from simply obeying God is the story of Naaman, the highly acclaimed captain of the Syrian army.

A. Naaman's Title and Reputation

The Bible describes Naaman as a great and honorable man, a "mighty man in valour." Although Naaman did not know it, the Lord had given Naaman his military victories. (See

II Kings 5:1; I Kings 22:15-17.) Naaman was notable among the people and demonstrated the kind of public character worthy of admiration. As a military man, there was none in his generation comparable to him. Yet, in spite of his great accomplishments and widespread acclaim, Naaman was a leper (II Kings 5:1).

B. Naaman's Affliction

Israelites considered lepers unclean. According to Jewish law they were not allowed to dwell in the presence of God. The Lord instructed Moses, "Command the children of Israel, that they put out of the camp every leper" (Numbers 5:2).

Leprosy is a powerful Old Testament representation of sin. What leprosy does to the outward person, sin does to the inward person. The prophet Isaiah graphically described the sinful people of Israel: "The whole head is sick, and the whole heart faint. From the sole of the foot even unto the head there is no soundness in it; but wounds, and bruises, and putrefying sores" (Isaiah 1:5-6). Just as leprosy caused a separation between lepers and others, sin causes a separation between mankind and his Maker. As Isaiah declared, "Your iniquities have separated between you and your God" (Isaiah 59:2).

Most people who have not obeyed the gospel do not like to think of themselves as spiritual lepers, but that is exactly the way God sees the unredeemed. Some may say, "I haven't done anything so bad." But the Bible asks, "Who can say, I have made my heart clean, I am pure from my sin?" (Proverbs 20:9). It declares, "All have sinned, and come short of the glory of God" (Romans 3:23). The unredeemed cannot see the repulsive deformities and sores with which sin has covered their inner being. Only Jesus can bring restoration and healing to a sin-sick soul.

II. THE UNKNOWN

A. The Maid's Title and Situation

The biblical narrative does not reveal the name of the lowly maiden who witnessed to her master's wife of the prophet in Israel. The Syrians had taken her captive in their latest campaign against Israel, and may have given her a Syrian name. It was her good fortune to be taken into the household of Naaman because his wife treated her kindly. The young maid missed her homeland, but it is clear she held her Syrian master and mistress in high esteem. She longed to see Naaman healed.

B. The Maid's Testimony

Although the general public may not have known about Naaman's dread disease, the servants in Naaman's household knew. Time passed while the Israelite maid worried about her master. One day she said to Naaman's wife, "Would God my lord were with the prophet that is in Samaria! for he would recover him of his leprosy" (II Kings 5:3). This showed remarkable faith because although there were many lepers in Israel during the time of Elisha, none of them had been healed. (See Luke 4:27.)

In many ways, the hero of this story is neither Naaman nor Elisha, but the little maid whose faith and compassion brought a message of hope to the household of a powerful and important man. We must be careful not to hold back at those key moments when God urges us to speak to others about His power.

III. THE PROPHET'S RESPONSE

Having heard about the possibility of a miraculous healing, Naaman repeated this to the king of Syria who said, "Go now, and I will send a letter to the king of Israel." Naaman packed his bags and departed for Samaria, about a hundred miles to the southwest.

King Joram rent his clothes when he read the message. "Does this Syrian think I'm God? Where did he get the idea I could heal his leprosy? He's trying to start another quarrel." Elisha happened to be in Samaria at the time and heard about the king's distress. He sent a message: "Tell the Syrian captain to come to me. He'll find out there's a prophet in Israel."

A. The Prophet Sent His Servant

Naaman stood at the prophet's door, expecting a distinguished man with healing powers to come out, call on his God, perform some kind of ritual, and heal his disease. It would be one great man healing another great man. Instead, the door opened and an ordinary man dressed in peasants' clothes stepped out. It was Elisha's messenger who relayed the message to Naaman: "Go and wash in Jordan seven times, and thy flesh shall come again to thee, and thou shalt be clean" (II Kings 5:10). Naaman's face turned red with rage. He had no intention of obeying the ridiculous command spoken by a common man.

Some people say they will not obey unless they hear directly from God. But ever since Moses emerged from the Midianite desert with a message of deliverance for Israel, God has conveyed His will to mankind through messengers—prophets and preachers.

B. The Prophet Voiced God's Rule

Paul explained the necessity of heeding the words of a preacher. "How then shall they call on him in whom they have not believed? and how shall they believe in him of whom they have not heard? and how shall they hear without a preacher?" (Romans 10:14). The solution for sin is to hear and obey the gospel of Jesus Christ.

IV. THE CAPTAIN'S RESPONSE

A. Naaman Insulted

The perceived snub infuriated Naaman. When his preconceived idea of how he would hear from God did not materialize, he concluded he had not heard from God. It was just some servant spouting ridiculous instructions.

Many today hear the words of a preacher and think them absurd. Self-exaltation does not let them see past the preacher's humanity and believe he is serving as a mouthpiece of God. Paul wrote, "Where is the disputer of this world? hath not God made foolish the wisdom of this world? For after that in the wisdom of God the world by wisdom knew not God, it pleased God by the foolishness of preaching to save them that believe" (I Corinthians 1:20-21). Paul was confident the words he spoke through divine inspiration were from God: "The gospel of Christ . . . is the power of God unto salvation to every one that believeth" (Romans 1:16).

B. Naaman's Rule

Naaman responded, "Are not Abana and Pharpar, rivers of Damascus, better than all the waters of Israel? may I not wash in them, and be clean?" (II Kings 5:12). In effect, Naaman was saying, "Why can't I be saved my own way? My way is better than God's way." But the Bible cautions, "There is a way that seemeth right unto a man, but the end thereof are the ways of death" (Proverbs 16:25). We are not in a position to tell God how to save us. He alone is "the author of eternal salvation unto all them that obey him" (Hebrews 5:9).

C. Naaman's Change of Heart

Once again, the words of a servant saved Naaman: "My father, if the prophet had bid thee do some great thing, wouldest thou not have done it? how much rather then, when he saith to thee, Wash, and be clean?" (II Kings 5:13). This gave Naaman pause. Maybe the man was right.

He swallowed his pride, turned around, went twenty-five miles to the banks of the muddy river, waded in, and began to dip. When he came up the seventh time, his flesh was clean and pure like that of a little child.

Paul preached that individuals should "repent and turn to God, and do works meet for repentance" (Acts 26:20). We know Naaman truly repented because he did exactly what the plan for healing required; he dipped in the Jordan. In the same way, a person's submission to water baptism in the name of Jesus Christ for the remission of sins is one of the only indisputable evidences that a person coming to God has repented of his sins.

D. Naaman's Healing and Cleansing

Naaman was healed by the grace of God. He neither earned nor deserved it. Naaman was healed because he responded to God's promise by acting in faith—by obeying God's instruction to dip in the Jordan. It would not have been enough for Naaman simply to confess, "I believe God will heal me" and go back to Damascus. In order for his faith to be effective, he actually had to follow through with what God had told Him to do. James expressed this idea: "Ye see then how that by works a man is justified, and not by faith only" (James 2:24).

Naaman's immersion by faith in the Jordan brought about cleansing from his leprosy. Our obedience to the Scriptures, including immersion by faith in the name of Jesus Christ, brings cleansing from our spiritual leprosy. Peter described it as the remission of sins (Acts 2:38). He later called it a blotting out of sins (Acts 3:19). Paul called it a washing away of sins and the forgiveness of sins (Acts 22:16; Colossians 1:14). But regardless of which term we use, it is always a gift of God's grace given to those who respond to the gospel in faithful obedience.

Internalizing the Message

Naaman showed his belief in the prophet's message by obeying the command to be immersed seven times in the Jordan. By doing this, he became for us an example of the power and blessing that comes to those who simply hear and obey the words of God. Whenever God's rule becomes our rule, the power of the miraculous begins to flow.

38

Lessons from History for Christian Living

The Certainty of Prophecy

week of 05.12.13

Lesson Text

II Kings 7:1-9

1 Then Elisha said, Hear ye the word of the LORD; Thus saith the LORD, To morrow about this time shall a measure of fine flour be sold for a shekel, and two measures of barley for a shekel, in the gate of Samaria.

2 Then a lord on whose hand the king leaned answered the man of God, and said, Behold, if the LORD would make windows in heaven, might this thing be? And he said, Behold, thou shalt see it with thine eyes, but shalt not eat thereof.

3 And there were four leprous men at the entering in of the gate: and they said one to another, Why sit we here until we die?

4 If we say, We will enter into the city, then the famine is in the city, and we shall die there: and if we sit still here, we die also. Now therefore come, and let us fall unto the host of the Syrians: if they save us alive, we shall live; and if they kill us, we shall but die.

5 And they rose up in the twilight, to go unto the camp of the Syrians: and when they were come to the uttermost part of the camp of Syria, behold, there was no man there.

6 For the Lord had made the host of the Syrians to hear a noise of chariots, and a noise of horses, even the noise of a great host: and they said one to another, Lo, the king of Israel hath hired against us the kings of the Hittites, and the kings of the Egyptians, to come upon us.

7 Wherefore they arose and fled in the twilight, and left their tents, and their horses, and their asses, even the camp as it was, and fled for their life.

8 And when these lepers came to the uttermost part of the camp, they went into one tent, and did eat and drink, and carried thence silver, and gold, and raiment, and went and hid it; and came again, and entered into another tent, and carried thence also, and went and hid it.

9 Then they said one to another, We do not well: this day is a day of good tidings, and we hold our peace: if we tarry till the morning light, some mischief will come upon us: now therefore come, that we may go and tell the king's household.

Focus Thought

The Word of God is replete with examples of fulfilled prophecy, the accuracy of which defies the law of probability.

Focus Verse

II Peter 1:19

We have also a more sure word of prophecy; whereunto ye do well that ye take heed, as unto a light that shineth in a dark place, until the day dawn, and the day star arise in your hearts.

39

Doing What You Can

by C. A. Brewer

The pictures I have seen of the Nazi concentration camps have left a lasting impression on me. The images of people starved to the point of death; the crematoriums, where the bodies of men, woman, and children were burned; the heaps of the dead, buried in mass graves, stagger my imagination. It is hard to comprehend how such barbaric cruelty could have taken place. And yet it did. In her book *Auschwitz: True Tales from a Grotesque Land*, Sara Nomberg-Prezytyk, once a prisoner at Auschwitz-Birkenau, the largest of the concentration camps, recounted how more than 1.1 million people, 90 percent of whom were Jews, were destroyed in that one camp.

But despite all the human depravity, there have been accounts of personal sacrifice and heroic efforts on the part of prisoners in these death camps. There are reports of inmates comforting inmates and sharing their last pieces of bread with others. There is no kindness like that displayed by those who themselves are in desperate need of kindness. In the worst of conditions, there are those who simply do what they can.

We may be tempted to think the little we do to help others is unimportant, that visiting a friend in a hospital, that praying for the parent with a wayward child, makes no significant difference. But Jesus commended the woman who poured out her costly ointment upon His head with the words, "She hath done what she could" (Mark 14:8).

Contemplating the Topic

The city of Samaria sprawled atop a three-hundred-foot hill. Its prominent location gave it a command of all of the major trade routes. Thirty years prior to the reign of Joram, King Omri had chosen the hilltop for his capital because of its natural defenses, but that did not stop Syria from trying to capture the city that sparkled like a jewel set in the fertile plain of Esdraelon.

Searching the Scriptures

I. THE LIMITATIONS OF MANKIND

A. A Plea for Justice

The siege rendered King Joram powerless against the Syrians and it frustrated him. One day as he assessed the situation from the top of the city wall, a woman approached and pleaded for help. He replied sarcastically, "And where will that help come from? Our busy threshing floors or overflowing winepresses? Everyone in the city is starving, woman." But she continued, "This woman promised me that if I would boil my son, we could eat him today and she would boil her son tomorrow. But she went back on her word and hid her son."

Appalled, the king tore his robe, revealing sackcloth underneath. (See II Kings 6:24-30.)

B. The Wrong Response

When people's hearts are not right with God, they turn to human solutions. In his twisted, backslidden state, King Joram failed to recognize the nearness of God and the effectiveness of fervent prayer. Instead of seeking the face of God with a repentant heart, Joram lashed out against the prophet of God, blaming him for their plight. "I'll have the head of Elisha the son of Shaphat today!"

C. A Certain Word

Elisha was sitting in his house with the elders when the word of the Lord came to him. He said, "Bar the door. The king has sent executioners to cut off my head, and he's following on their heels to see it done." When the king arrived he accused, "You call yourself a prophet. What good has it done to wait upon the Lord for help? He hasn't helped us yet. He's the one who sent this calamity in the first place." (See II Kings 6:32-33.)

Elisha was not intimidated. He did not try to defend himself. He declared, "Thus saith the LORD, To morrow about this time shall a measure of fine flour be sold for a shekel, and two measures of barley for a shekel, in the gate of Samaria" (II Kings 7:1). Impossible!

40

None of the hungry people who heard this, not even the elders, could imagine how Elisha's words could come to pass. The king's right-hand man scoffed, "Even if the Lord opens the floodgates of Heaven, *that* will never happen. Everyone in Samaria knows that only yesterday a donkey head was selling for eighty pieces of silver, and a fourth part of dove's dung for five pieces of silver." (See II Kings 7:2; 6:25.)

II. FULFILLMENT OF PROPHECY

A. The Impossible

Impossibilities become the media for miracles. Everyone faces situations that are impossible from a human perspective. It might be the salvation of a spouse or a wayward child; it might be a dire financial situation; it might be an incurable disease; it might be a relational problem in a family or a church. We sometimes feel compelled to give God instructions as to how to accomplish what He has promised, but God's promises will surely come to pass—usually in ways we have never considered.

B. Providence

Throughout the siege Ben-hadad had thought he was in control. But now he and his army were on the run, chased by a federation of Hittites, Egyptians, and Israelites—or so they assumed. King Joram had thought he was in control when he was crowned king. But he sat helpless in his ivory palace waiting for starvation to kill him before the Syrians did. Neither king could control the events God had set in motion. Even before Elisha uttered his prophetic words, the providence of God had been planning and executing the works that would turn the hopeless situation into a miraculous victory and joyful feasting for Samaria.

God has not changed. No matter how impossible our situation seems, if God makes a promise, it will come to pass no matter how others may scoff or try to hinder—and no matter how much we worry and try to help out God.

III. THE DAY OF GOOD NEWS

"Wait a minute," said one of the lepers. The others paused, their arms loaded with treasures. "We're not doing right. There's more stuff in this camp than we could use in ten lifetimes. What about the people in Samaria who are still starving? What about our own families? This is the best day of our lives. If we keep everything for ourselves, even if it's just overnight, Providence might punish us and put us in a worse state than we were before. We need to tell the king what we've found."

A. We Are Not Doing Right

When we came to God, we experienced the best thing that ever happened to us. We freely received salvation, love, contentment, help in time of need, fellowship with the saints, all the spiritual food and drink we could want—God lavished everything upon us. But like the people in Samaria, the world sits in darkness, starving for what we have and longing for deliverance from their desperate situation. Why should we leave our treasures and go tell them the good news? What did they ever do for us except ridicule, persecute, and despitefully use us? We should do it not only for the people's sake and for Christ's sake, but also for our own.

B. Go and Tell

We too have a responsibility to go and tell the good news of deliverance through Jesus Christ to starving people huddling behind the gates. Jesus Himself commanded us to take the good news to everyone. (See Matthew 28:18-19.) We can rest assured that when we share the good news in the power of the Holy Ghost, God will have been working ahead of time to remove the enemy and clear the way for the gospel. Paul asked for the prayers of the Thessalonians that He would not be hindered in spreading the gospel.

Internalizing the Message

This story holds many valuable lessons for us.
• Humans have many limitations; with God, however, the possibilities are endless.
• Instead of lashing out at God or the man of God because of calamity, we should repent and ask God for help.
• When a message from God arrives, instead of scoffing at the apparent impossibility, we should begin to look for the remedy He supplies. Scoffers will not be there to enjoy the rewards.
• Freely we have received good news, spiritual food and drink, and treasures from God. We should readily tell others the good news about what God has to offer.
• The treasures do not belong to us; they belong to God.

12 The Half-Hearted Effort

week of
05.19.13

Lesson Text

II Kings 13:14-19

14 Now Elisha was fallen sick of his sickness whereof he died. And Joash the king of Israel came down unto him, and wept over his face, and said, O my father, my father, the chariot of Israel, and the horsemen thereof.

15 And Elisha said unto him, Take bow and arrows. And he took unto him bow and arrows.

16 And he said to the king of Israel, Put thine hand upon the bow. And he put his hand upon it: and Elisha put his hands upon the king's hands.

17 And he said, Open the window eastward. And he opened it. Then Elisha said, Shoot. And he shot. And he said, The arrow of the LORD'S deliverance, and the arrow of deliverance from Syria: for thou shalt smite the Syrians in Aphek, till thou have consumed them.

18 And he said, Take the arrows. And he took them. And he said unto the king of Israel, Smite upon the ground. And he smote thrice, and stayed.

19 And the man of God was wroth with him, and said, Thou shouldest have smitten five or six times; then hadst thou smitten Syria till thou hadst consumed it: whereas now thou shalt smite Syria but thrice.

Galatians 5:7

7 Ye did run well; who did hinder you that ye should not obey the truth?

Focus Thought

A half-hearted effort will never bring the complete victory God plans for His people.

Focus Verse

Matthew 11:12

And from the days of John the Baptist until now the kingdom of heaven suffereth violence, and the violent take it by force.

Persistent Faith

by C. A. Brewer

A popular gospel song from the past states, "Prayer is the key to Heaven, but faith unlocks the door." While there is certainly truth in these words, something else could be added. It is not feeble faith or wavering faith that opens the way into the presence of God. It is bold, persistent faith that makes the difference. It is often knocking at the door over and over until the answer arrives.

Persistent faith is like the widow petitioning the unjust judge day after day until he became bone weary of her coming. Unrelenting faith is like Elijah on top of Carmel praying "until"—until his servant saw the cloud the size of a man's hand, the portent of a mighty downpour on a desperately dry land. Importunate faith is like the man who went to his friend's house at midnight and pounded on the door until he received the three loaves he needed.

Motivational speakers of our day often encourage their listeners to persistently believe in themselves, instructing them, "You can do anything you want to do." The truth, however, lies not in what we can do on our own. It lies in what we will believe God to do in and through us. Jesus said, "If ye have faith as a grain of mustard seed, ye shall say unto this mountain, Remove hence to yonder place; and it shall remove; and nothing shall be impossible unto you" (Matthew 17:20).

Contemplating the Topic

Those who seek to know God for the value of the relationship itself, who obey His Word in good times and bad, usually develop a passion for God that casual observers can never understand. That passion compels them to follow the voice of God even when He demands things that seem pointless or unnecessary. It is as if they, like Jeremiah, have a fire burning inside that demands to be freed and they can shout with the prophet, "But His word was in my heart like a burning fire shut up in my bones; I was weary of holding it back, and I could not" (Jeremiah 20:9, NKJV). That passion forces entrance into a realm where service and obedience become passageways into holy places not accessible by humanly devised means.

Searching the Scriptures

I. DISTURBING DISTRACTIONS

A. Prophet's Sickness

Every person has an appointment with death (Hebrews 9:27). While the condition promised is the same for us all, God chooses various ways to transport us there. Regardless of how it is accomplished, the passing of a child of God from this life into the next is care-fully observed in Heaven. "Precious in the sight of the LORD is the death of his saints" (Psalm 116:15). God chose an illness to carry His servant Elisha home. Elisha may have been one of the Old Testament heroes the writer was thinking of when he wrote, "These all died in faith" (Hebrews 11:13).

B. King's Affection

Joash, like all of the Northern Kingdom of Israel's kings before and after him, reigned in sin and disobedience, refusing to turn from the sinful path his father had chosen (II Kings 13:11). But even in his sinfulness, Joash recognized the impact of Elisha's ministry on Israel. When he learned of the prophet's sickness, Joash went to visit him.

C. Victim of His Grief

Grief is a process a person must move through. Without an understanding of God's eternal plan and the knowledge our heart is right in His sight, grief ends in misery. "If in this life only we have hope in Christ, we are of all men most miserable" (I Corinthians 15:19). Because Joash had no relationship with God, the pending death of Elisha compounded his grief.

II. PROPHET'S CONCERN

A. Focus on the Problem

Both men stood at a critical crossroads. The prophet was sick and knew his life was almost over. Israel's existence was threatened and the king had no viable solution for its preservation. One would expect hope and encouragement to come from the younger man who had much of his life still before him and all of his country's resources at his disposal. Yet the dying man was the one with the link to hope. Although death was looming over him, Elisha's commitment to God's Word provided a connection with God that even sickness and death could not sever.

B. Look to the Future

Without as much as a gentle segue, the prophet interrupted the king's weeping, demanding he fetch a bow and some arrows. As Elisha placed his hand over Joash's, he commanded the king to shoot an arrow toward the east, the direction from which his enemies had come. As the arrow flew, the prophet declared, "The arrow of the LORD'S deliverance, and the arrow of deliverance from Syria: for thou shalt smite the Syrians in Aphek, till thou have consumed them" (II Kings 13:17).

III. KING'S HALF-HEARTEDNESS

A. Lack of Desperation

After commanding Joash to shoot an arrow toward the east, Elisha told him to take some arrows and strike the ground. Joash hit the ground three times and stopped. His passionless motion angered Elisha. "Thou shouldest have smitten five or six times" (II Kings 13:19).

B. Enemy Not Eliminated

The king's half-hearted obedience disappointed the prophet. Only because of God's promise to Abraham, Isaac, and Jacob was Joash granted a reprieve from his enemies (II Kings 13:23). But because of his lack of passionate involvement with God's Word, Israel's victory would be only temporary (II Kings 13:19).

IV. DELIVERANCE FOR THE WHOLEHEARTED

A. Staying Focused

At the conclusion of Elisha's ministry, when Joash came to visit, Elisha did not allow his sickness to distract him from the message God had given him to deliver. His own comfort and well-being would be considered only after he had discharged the task God had assigned. Even as he faced death, Elisha kept his heart focused on the Word of God.

B. Acting Aggressively

Nothing we read of Jesus' earthly ministry or the actions of first-century Christians suggests that God's twenty-first-century church should be passive, deferring to the collective wisdom of popular logic. Instead, His church should have the passion of Elisha, realizing that even death is no threat to the promises and power of God. "From the days of John the Baptist until now the kingdom of heaven suffereth violence, and the violent take it by force" (Matthew 11:12). Weak and timid attempts will be unsuccessful in the church Jesus is building.

The Word of God frequently requires action that those unfamiliar with His methods may find confusing or pointless. Just as Joash may have felt foolish striking the ground with the arrows, we may find God's instructions to be somewhat strange and unfamiliar in our present situation. However, we must be aggressive and unafraid to follow God outside our comfort zone. Total victory awaits those who passionately interact with God's Word.

C. Refusing to Give Up

Life offers little to those unwilling to struggle. God's promises do not apply to those who will not fight to receive them. Tenacity and determination are essential for every Christian's success.

Elisha had been promised a double portion of Elijah's spirit, yet more than four decades had passed since he had last ministered in the king's presence. But during those forty quiet years, Elisha's commitment remained and his devotion to the Word of God did not waver. When the time came for one last message to Israel, the old prophet, though out of the limelight for years, did not miss a beat. He never lost faith in the God who called him; therefore, his God never failed the one He had called.

Internalizing the Message

God hates insipid indifference. "So then because thou art lukewarm, and neither cold nor hot, I will spue thee out of my mouth" (Revelation 3:16). A passionless believer simply going through the motions may be blessed because of God's covenant with his fathers, but he will have no spiritual heritage to pass on to his own children. At best his victories, like Joash's, will be temporary pauses in his enemy's march to total domination. Every believer should earnestly pursue a passionate relationship with God.

44

Lost and Found

13
week of
05.26.13

Lesson Text

II Kings 22:8-13, 18-20

8 And Hilkiah the high priest said unto Shaphan the scribe, I have found the book of the law in the house of the LORD. And Hilkiah gave the book to Shaphan, and he read it.

9 And Shaphan the scribe came to the king, and brought the king word again, and said, Thy servants have gathered the money that was found in the house, and have delivered it into the hand of them that do the work, that have the oversight of the house of the LORD.

10 And Shaphan the scribe shewed the king, saying, Hilkiah the priest hath delivered me a book. And Shaphan read it before the king.

11 And it came to pass, when the king had heard the words of the book of the law, that he rent his clothes.

12 And the king commanded Hilkiah the priest, and Ahikam the son of Shaphan, and Achbor the son of Michaiah, and Shaphan the scribe, and Asahiah a servant of the king's, saying,

13 Go ye, inquire of the LORD for me, and for the people, and for all Judah, concerning the words of this book that is found: for great is the wrath of the LORD that is kindled against us, because our fathers have not hearkened unto the words of this book, to do according unto all that which is written concerning us.

. . . . .

18 But to the king of Judah which sent you to inquire of the LORD, thus shall ye say to him, Thus saith the LORD God of Israel, As touching the words which thou hast heard;

19 Because thine heart was tender, and thou hast humbled thyself before the LORD, when thou heardest what I spake against this place, and against the inhabitants thereof, that they should become a desolation and a curse, and hast rent thy clothes, and wept before me; I also have heard thee, saith the LORD.

20 Behold therefore, I will gather thee unto thy fathers, and thou shalt be gathered into thy grave in peace; and thine eyes shall not see all the evil which I will bring upon this place. And they brought the king word again.

Focus Thought

God's Word is precious, and we should value it as an integral and vital part of our lives.

Focus Verse

Luke 15:8

Either what woman having ten pieces of silver, if she lose one piece, doth not light a candle, and sweep the house, and seek diligently till she find it?

Buried Treasures
by Richard M. Davis

Although metal detectors have been around for quite some time, I remember when less expensive detectors became commonly popular. It seemed they were appearing everywhere, and along with their appearance were people of all sorts, shapes, and sizes—in parks, on beaches, on vacant lots—diligently looking for buried treasures. To be sure, most of them were not looking for the treasures left behind by pirates or thieves. As adventurous as that thought may be, in a lifetime most of us will never discover treasures left behind by pirates. Rather, these adventurers sought lost coins or other metal artifacts that might have had value due to their historic or antique qualities. When metal detectors became readily available, many individuals instantly became treasure hunters.

Although I found the metal detectors and their operators fascinating, I never owned a detector and I never had the opportunity to use one. By now, however, others may already have found all the really "good stuff."

I am a treasure hunter, however. There is no treasure greater than the Word of God. In the Bible are a multitude of buried treasures that only require extraction—someone willing to take the time to "dig them out" for himself.

As revealed in our lesson today, the Bible is full of buried treasures that are continually fresh and relevant to every generation of believers. Within its holy and sacred pages we may discover enlightenment through spiritual illumination. The treasures from the Bible bring wisdom and understanding through careful study. And best of all, its treasures bring opportunity for salvation and revival.

Are you a treasure hunter? You can find many invaluable treasures buried in God's Word.

Contemplating the Topic

God's expressed Word, which we have through the Holy Bible, is His revelation of Himself. To whatever extent a human can comprehend God, his understanding of God stands primarily and foremost upon the Word of God, which reveals Him to mankind. Consequently, there is nothing more valuable than God's Word.

Even though God exceeds mankind's ability to fully comprehend Him, we can understand that which God has chosen to reveal to us about Himself. Further, what God has chosen to reveal to us is adequate to form the foundation for us to have a relationship with Him. We can learn these self-revelations of God through the study of His Holy Word. What an invaluable Book!

Searching the Scriptures

How frustrating it must have been to some of the people of God to recognize they had lost something of great value when they lost God's Word! Others, however, were blind to the loss for they failed to grasp its true value. All, however, suffered from the loss of God's Word. The loss was theirs to suffer together as a nation.

I. BOOK OF THE LAW LOST

A. Exhibited Carelessness toward the Law

God's Word was revered in Israel during the reign of Solomon. However, after his reign and the subsequent division of the kingdom, both the Northern Kingdom, Israel, and the Southern Kingdom, Judah, faltered in their faith. Israel faltered altogether and was carried away into captivity, never to return as a nation. Judah also faltered but experienced occasional revivals. One such revival in Judah occurred under King Hezekiah.

At age twenty-five Hezekiah became king of Judah. Hezekiah's first agenda item was to abolish idolatry, including the brazen serpent, an icon God used for a purpose but which He never intended to become an object of worship. Hezekiah restored Temple worship at a time when the doors to the Temple may have been literally closed. (See II Chronicles 29:3, 7.) Hezekiah had a strong faith in God and was particularly interested in collecting and arranging sacred writings, including some proverbs (Proverbs 25:1) and possibly some psalms (II Chronicles 29:30).

Rather than choosing to follow politically correct options, Hezekiah opted to keep his faith securely anchored in God. "And the LORD was with him; and he prospered whithersoever he went forth: and he rebelled against the king of Assyria, and served him not" (II Kings 18:7). In 701 BC Hezekiah's faith repelled the assault of the Assyrians. Even so, Hezekiah also eventually experienced a backsliding in his faith and relationship with God.

In 687 BC, Manasseh began his half-century reign of decline. During his reign idols were set up in the Temple and worshiped alongside Jehovah. The king practiced divination and encouraged the sacrificing of children to Moloch. "Moreover Manasseh shed innocent blood very much, till he had filled Jerusalem from one end to another; beside his sin wherewith he made Judah to sin, in doing that which was evil in the sight of the LORD" (II Kings 21:16). Manasseh is traditionally credited with the murder of the prophet Isaiah. Interestingly, he reigned longer than any king in Judah. His son Amon succeeded Manasseh as king but soon was assassinated.

During this terrible time in the history of Judah, the people became careless with regard to their religious duty. They certainly were religious, but they had forgotten about the worship of the one true God. Their regard for God's Word so greatly diminished that they lost the written scrolls of the Law. In a time when documents were handwritten and copies were not abundant, the Law literally was out of sight—and unfortunately out of mind.

B. Ignored the Law

The only way to lose a scroll that once was revered and used in ritual worship was for it to be devalued and no longer used in worship. The attitude of the people toward God's Word placed it in a secondary position to other beliefs and to new traditions. As a result, moral decline and degeneracy set in.

Ignoring God's Word is a sure path away from God. Knowing God's revelation about Himself and His desires for humankind is the only way to know Him; that requires knowing His Word. When we depart from God's Word, we depart from God.

C. Avoided Its Condemning Contents

Ignoring God's Word may allow us to remove from our consciousness the demands of God's Word. However, just because we remove God's Word from our lives does not mean we remove the demands of God's Word. To will-ingly disobey God's Word or to ignorantly neglect His Word makes us guilty before God. Religious duty and ritual can never compensate for ignoring God's Word. Religious duty without adherence to God's Word is without value. Religious duty and ritual can never substitute for obedience to God's Word.

Judah was never more religious than during this time when the Law was lost, but they fell far short of pleasing God. They worshiped many gods and exercised vibrant rituals, but they were far from God.

Without God's Word, worship only spirals away from God. There is no relationship with God apart from His Word.

II. BOOK FOUND

At age sixteen Josiah began to seek the Lord. His initial reform consisted of repairing the Temple and abolishing idolatry. His quest for renewal was more than just a prayer; he began personally to repent and initiate within the kingdom steps of repentance to restore his and Judah's relationship with God.

Although sincerity alone is insufficient, God honors sincerity, and "he is a rewarder of them that diligently seek him" (Hebrews 11:6). As Josiah sought to restore Israel's religion and worship of the one true God, He honored Josiah's diligence. In a subsequent wave of reforms in 622 BC, Josiah's workers found Moses' law book in the Temple. What a treasure to rediscover the Law! Their discovery would enlighten them to a host of oversights on the part of all the people of Judah, which had led them to a position of sinful disobedience and away from relationship with the Almighty.

The effects of all these reforms apparently reached beyond Judah into Israel. (See II Chronicles 34:6.)

III. KING'S RESPONSE

The first reaction God's Word causes in a sincere believer is repentance. When a person believes the Bible is God's Word and he sincerely desires to please God, he desires to obey the Word. When the Word shines the light of truth upon his errant ways, it produces condemnation and contrition within the heart of the believer, which initiate repentance. Such was the case when King Josiah heard the reading of the Book of the Law.

Faith in the Law caused the king to spring into immediate action:

1. He repented personally (II Kings 22:11-20).

2. He gathered all the people together and had the Word read in their hearing (II Kings 23:1-2).

3. He covenanted with the Lord to obey the Word (II Kings 23:3).

4. He cleared out all the vessels of idol worship from the Temple and had them burned (II Kings 23:4).

5. He cleared out and destroyed all other elements of idol worship, perversion, and defilement (II Kings 23:5-19).

6. He caused the idolatrous priests to be slain (II Kings 23:20).

7. He reinstated the Passover (II Kings 23:21-23).

8. He began to perform all the words of the Law and serve God with all his heart so that he was unlike any king before or after him (II Kings 23:24-25).

God's Word never loses its power! It will produce results in the hearts of those who hear it and obey it.

God's Word will accomplish its divine mission, one way or another.

IV. BIBLE AS VALUED TREASURE

A. Is Always Fresh and Relevant

God's Word abides even when it is lost to us! It does not change. It does not dissipate. It is forever settled in Heaven. Our neglect of God's Word does not diminish it one bit. Jesus said, "For verily I say unto you, Till heaven and earth pass, one jot or one tittle shall in no wise pass from the law, till all be fulfilled" (Matthew 5:18). When we recover God's Word and restore it to its rightful place in our lives, it again will prove to be as effective and powerful as ever.

God's Word is never outdated, outmoded, or irrelevant. It will provide direction and understanding for every situation. Times change and people change, but their fundamental needs are forever the same.

B. Provides Enlightenment through Spiritual Illumination

Sometimes we speak of the Bible giving *revelation*, which is certainly true in a sense; however, perhaps *illumination* is a more appropriate term. The Bible's principles are not new, though they may be new to us as individuals. We just need divine illumination to shine upon the principles of God so we may see them and understand them. That is what the Bible does for people in every generation. It opens to their understanding the timeless principles of God so

they may have the opportunity to understand and embrace them.

C. Brings Wisdom and Understanding through Study

The wisdom and understanding provided in the Scriptures do not come by osmosis or mere contact; they come through prayerful study. We are to put forth effort to learn what God desires to communicate to us through His Word.

D. Brings Salvation and Revival

The Word of God is the roadmap to redemption. While it is true that the Bible itself cannot save us, it contains the words of truth that reveal the only means of salvation. From the Book of Genesis to the final Book of Revelation, God's Word was either laying foundation and pointing toward Jesus Christ, or pointing back to the supreme sacrifice He made on the cross for the redemption of souls from sin. Ultimately, it is all about salvation through Jesus Christ!

Internalizing the Message

The spiritual decline and experiences of the two kingdoms of Israel and Judah should serve both as a warning and a motivation to all true believers in Jesus Christ. Their exhibited examples clearly reveal the end results when either a nation or an individual becomes careless toward God's Word and the spiritual laws it communicates. The people became bored with the Book of the Law and careless toward its truths. Further, they began to ignore the parts that caused them to feel condemnation and discomfort. They failed to understand, however, that their avoidance of the Law did not annul its truths or its judgment of their guilt. May we learn from their severe mistake.

They came to understand the true treasure of having God's Word actively guiding and directing their lives. They discovered its fresh relevance for directing their paths, and they came to appreciate the enlightenment they received through the spiritual illumination it brought. Most of all, they rediscovered the wisdom of its truths that brought revival and salvation to their nation and lives.

These are vital lessons for believers today! Our only hope of revival and redemption come through God's Word. May we always treasure its active place in our lives and obey its life-giving principles that we may be saved.